DARK JUSTICE
WHITE COLLAR
CRIMES

DARK JUSTICE
WHITE COLLAR CRIMES

GAETANO PICCADACI

EXTREME OVERFLOW PUBLISHING

EXTREME OVERFLOW PUBLISHING
A Brand of Extreme Overflow Enterprises, Inc.
P.O. Box 1811
Dacula, GA 30019
www.extremeoverflow.com

Copyright © 2024 Gaetano Piccadaci. All rights reserved.

No part of this book may be reproduced or transmitted in any form or by any means electronic or mechanical photocopying, recording, or by any information storage and retrieval system without the prior written permission of the author, except for the inclusion of brief quotations in critical reviews and certain other noncommercial uses permitted by copyright law.

Re-Published by Extreme Overflow Publishing
Produced by GP Entertainment Enterprises

Printed in the United States of America
Library of Congress Catalog in-Publication
Data is available for this title

For permission requests, contact the publisher.
Send feedback to info@extremeoverflow.com

CONTENTS

Prologue	9
Chapter 1: Starting a Business	12
Chapter 2: A New Job	17
Chapter 3: The Unthinkable	23
Chapter 4: Spring Time	31
Chapter 5: May, June & College	39
Chapter 6: July, August & Job Ending	45
Chapter 7: Finding an Attorney	51
Chapter 8: Second Attorney	59
Chapter 9: The Letter	67
Chapter 10: Medication & Mental Stress	73
Chapter 11: Primary Care	79
Chapter 12: Therapy	87
Chapter 13: More Therapy	95
Chapter 14: Writing Letters and Reporting Crimes	105
Chapter 15: Doctor Visits	111
Chapter 16: C.D.C.	119
Chapter 17: Social Security	127
Chapter 18: Deposition	135
Chapter 19: Second Deposition	143
Chapter 20: Family & White Collar Crimes	153
Chapter 21: Workmen's Compensation	159
Chapter 22: Judge Decision	167
Chapter 23: Rip-Off	173
Chapter 24: Meeting a Friend	183

Chapter 25: Government, Laws & the C.D.C.	191
Chapter 26: Primary Doctor & the C.D.C.	199
Chapter 27: Attorney Allen	207
Chapter 28: Independent Contractors	215
Chapter 29: Private Investigator	225
Chapter 30: Letter to the New Judge	231
Chapter 31: Resending Letters	237
Chapter 32: God and Religion	245
Chapter 33: Mental Abuse and Fibromyalgia	253
Chapter 34: Standing Alone	259
Chapter 35: The Challenges	267
Chapter 36: The Media	271
Chapter 37: History of Mankind	275
Chapter 38: Final Health Problems Summary	281
Chapter 39: Final Thoughts	287

Dark Justice White Collar Crimes

PROLOGUE

This story is a true account of a man who tried to achieve success in a corrupt world. Some of the people involved worked at the town level. Others were doctors, lawyers, judges, and state politicians. Revolving around corruption in a small town, stage governments, medical communities, among the other professional people who were also corrupt led a good man to a life that would never be the same.

The main character started a successful career running his own business and then went on to work for a town. His goal was to retire from his town job. Unfortunately, a turn of events changed this man's life forever. He endured multiple issues involving his health, legal matters, family problems, and financial issues.

The sharp turn events began to shift when a boss who was a superintendent at the time, bullied everybody on the job. He is guilty of verbal abuse, racial discrimination, and many other indiscretions that can be proven. The abuse this man suffered was so severe, it was also carried out by medical doctors, attorneys, the legal system, and politicians who seemed to all be working with each other toward the common interest of self gain. The mental torture from this level of pain is easy to feel but very hard to explain. Plus, the side effects of any mental stress condition caused physical issues that can stop anyone from leading a normal everyday life.

The federal and state laws in our country are supposed to control the criminal action of white-collar crimes committed by professional people and legal authorities, but nobody wanted to hear this man's truth about the severity of these problems when this heartbroken man tried to complain through the proper legal channels. White-collar crimes don't seem to carry any weight in the eyes of the law until a serious problem occurs that effects them. In a one-on-one situation, a common person who has a valid complaint doesn't seem to have a fighting chance against the medical and legal systems of this country. The silver lining is that the story can still be told.

This story exposes the true account of the corruption, and the criminals (medical and legal professionals and legal authorities) involved with the dark justice of white-collar crimes.

The story is true; all names of places and people have been changed for copyright and legal reasons.

CHAPTER 1
Starting a Business

In 1980, I entered my sophomore year at Yellow Hills Regional High School, where I excelled as an honor student across all classes, with a particular passion for carpentry shop. My journey into the workforce began at the age of fourteen with a paper route, and over time, I took on various roles in carpentry, lawn care, yard cleaning, and other odd jobs. These experiences laid the foundation for understanding the significance of sound business ethics. In my carpentry business, I not only honed my craft but also knew business planning, accounting, and office management.

As my career progressed, I took on more significant projects that demanded a heightened sense of responsibility towards myself, my clients, and my team. Diligence and dedication resulted in a string of satisfied customers, culminating in my graduation from Yellow Hills Regional High School in 1982. Guided by my father's wisdom and collaboration, I started on my own business, Vincent D'Angelo Jr. Construction.

My father, Vincent D'Angelo Sr., and my mother, Maria D'Angelo, instilled in me the traditional Sicilian values of respect, loyalty, pride, and honesty. Growing up in a close-knit family, I, as the eldest of four siblings; after me came Joseph, Sarah Maria, and Anthony. We all understood the importance of common sense, education, and striving for excellence. The lessons learned from school, life, and business were absorbed to the best of my ability, and I became a sponge, always seeking knowledge.

After two years in the business post-graduation, it was time to expand my businesses. I obtained a builder's license, insurance, a new truck with a plow, and toolboxes with an array of different tools. I got an accountant, set up bank accounts, and other details to ensure the legality of my business. The journey wasn't without challenges, as the economic landscape dictated the rhythm of both good and bad times. I learned the lesson of inconsistency in business the hard way because nobody can predict the future economy. When the economic problems started, I had to let go of good workers. When times got better, I tried to rehire them. Sometimes they would reply that they had already found other jobs. My father's steadfast advice to keep fighting echoed in my ears as I confronted the challenges that came my way. In time, I received a commercial driving license and a hoisting license. These license's opened up newer and bigger jobs for my company and me. The idea was to cross-train with all different aspects of construction. The more I improved myself, the higher the price of doing business went. It seemed that the working person was always behind the eight ball. My father always advised me to keep trying and to never give up or give in to problems no matter how big or small. He told me to keep fighting.

Embracing the winter season, I invested in a new truck with a plow, aligning residential contracts and subcontracting snowplowing with the town of Butland in the DPW office in October 2002. Simultaneously, I submitted a job application for full-time employment, setting the stage for a transformative chapter in my career.

Eleven years as a subcontractor for the DPW office, marked by accolades for my snowplowing work, paved the way for a remarkable opportunity. Enduring the harshest winter conditions, I diligently plowed the streets for the DPW office over a span of eleven years as a subcontractor. Simultaneously, I managed my construction business, juggling the demands of both roles. My dedication to excellence in snowplowing didn't go unnoticed; residents of Butland showered me with compliments, as did the town itself and my supervisor, Superintendent Robert Smith. Recognizing my proficiency, Smith consistently designated me as the first subcontractor to be called after all town workers were on the job.

In October 2013, a call from the town presented the chance for a permanent full-time position. The interview process, physical examination, and drug test unfolded seamlessly, culminating in a job offer that I eagerly expressed my interest towards.

During the call, the DPW secretary explained the interview process. First, there would be an interview with Superintendent Robert Smith, Assistant Supervisor Jimmy Flynn, and Assistant Supervisor Chuck Freedman. Then there would be a physical and a drug test. I agreed with the secretary's explanation of the process and we set up an appointment for an interview. It was to be on October 26, 2013. When I showed up for the interview, I exchanged greetings with Robert Smith. He asked me to sit in the other room and wait for the other bosses. I went to take a seat, and Smith said, "You took my chair. What are you trying to do, take over my job?"

I told him I didn't know he was sitting there, and he told me he was sitting there, and I should sit at the other end of the table.

When the meeting started, Smith introduced everyone. Then he said that we needed to conduct the meeting as a formality even though he knew that we all knew each other. I agreed with his plan. Smith then asked all the questions. First he asked how long I had been in business. I said since 1980. Then he asked how long I had been working for the town as a subcontractor. I said about eleven years. Then he asked which high school I had attended. I said Yellow Hill Regional High, Banton, Rhode Island.

Smith then asked how my grades in school had been. And I said that I was an A and B student. He asked what year I graduated, and I said 1982. That caused Smith to observe that I had started my business in 1980 and graduated in 1982. How could that be? I was only sixteen years old.

I told them that I had been working with my father since I was eight years old, and then I went to high school. I also said that I learned at a very fast pace in my carpentry shop. My teachers could not believe how easy carpentry was for me. I was the best in my business in carpentry and construction. Smith then asked why I was coming to the town for a job.

I told him that I loved my business and the work, but running it and maintaining it came at a very high price. I worked twenty-four hours a day, seven days a week. And the costs and challenges were too high for me to continue. I was getting older and wanted to work a forty-hour week instead of all the time.

Smith asked if I was willing to give up the money I earned in my business for a job that paid a lot less.

I told him I had money. I just wanted to have a regular job with benefits and regular hours. He asked if I planned to continue to work at my business part time, but I said I wasn't. My company required too much dedication to the work itself, the customers, and the workers."

He told me that he liked the fact that I had been dedicated to my job and the people involved in my life. He said he would like to hire me if the two assistant supervisors agreed. The two assistant supervisors then agreed with Smith's decision. They also said that I would be a great asset to the town and the job. Smith said he would hire me if I passed a physical and a drug test. I told him that wouldn't be a problem. I knew I didn't use drugs, and I was physically fit.

All the bosses agreed, and the meeting ended. The two assistants then left the office, and Smith asked me to stay because he wanted to talk to me as a friend. He asked me to sit down so he could talk to me. I asked him what he needed. He said he knew I had been there for some time as a subcontractor, but he needed to explain how things work around there. When I asked what he meant, he told me that I already knew most of the guys—the workers. He knew I was friends with them. Then he said that he needed a person he could trust who could report to him about the guys and what they were saying about work or anything else that he needed to know about.

I told him we had a problem because I wasn't the sort of guy who snitched on anyone. I believed in obeying my bosses, but I drew the line with this demand or request. I reminded him that I had been a boss myself, and I had never asked anyone to do what he was asking me to do. I told him he had the wrong guy. I said I was there to work and put in my time till I retired. Then I asked if this was going to stop me from being hired.

Smith said that my response wouldn't jeopardize the opportunity I had with his office; he had just been asking me to do him a favor. I told him he would have to do his own dirty work, and he said okay; we didn't have a problem. He told me to report to the doctor's office the next day, and we would see if I could pass the physical and drug test."

The next day, after the physical and drug test, the doctor explained that I had passed the physical, but the results of the drug test would take a couple of days. I thanked him. A couple of days passed, and I received a call from the town explaining that I had a job. The DPW secretary asked when I could start, and I said, "The sooner, the better."

She said she wanted me to begin on Monday, November 2, 2013, and I agreed. I passed this information on to my family members, and they were all happy for me. I had a new job with the town of Butland.

Regrettably, my father, Vincent D'Angelo Sr., had passed away in 1998 due to mesothelioma, a consequence of asbestos exposure. While my father was no longer with us, He would never get to see that I was following his steps working for the state of Rhode Island.

CHAPTER 2

A New Job

The first day on the job with the town of Butland was a very good day for me because I was starting a normal life for myself. The day began at 7:00 in the morning and ended at 3:30 in the afternoon. The atmosphere buzzed with camaraderie whenever my coworkers joked around with me. They'd say, I'd finally made it to the DPW office of Butland. They were pleased that I was working for the town because they already knew that my work habits and character would be a good match for the demands of the job.

I was assigned to the garbage trucks department. Each truck required one driver and two laborers (trash collectors). This department was also under the highway department. The highway foreman for this department was Scott Craw. The guys explained the week's routine working with the garbage trucks. On Mondays and Fridays we had the longest routes for garbage in Butland. Tuesdays, Wednesdays, and Thursdays were shorter days, so one of the trucks would not have to go out after lunch on the short days, and the three men would be assigned to another job that needed to be done in the DPW office.

The chilling cold weather started in November, so I asked Smith why he had started me in the cold months. His response bore the weight of curiosity, as He stated that he wanted to know if I was telling the truth about working through the winter. Plus, lots of guys failed in the winter because of winters frigid grip, plowing mountains of snow, and working around the clock. It was common for workers to plow all night and work all day at their regular assignments. I asked if we could actually work for forty-eight hours straight if we had a massive snowstorm. Smith replied yes, if not longer than that. He reminded me there would also be clean-up at the town square and other places. Smith also explained that, when a new job opened up within the department, I should sign in for that job. He said that the other workers would get mad at me because workers needed to be there a year before they were even thought of for that job, and then the experience and time would also matter.

When each day started at 7:00 in the morning, all the workers keeping as warm as possible in thick construction coats, long John pants and thick socks under our boots, attended roll call and received job assignments. The first was the garbage trucks and crews—three trucks and three men to a truck. The second was the recycling truck with two men; this was considered part of the garbage brigade. The third was the mechanic shop. The fourth was repair jobs and checking pipelines for the water and sewer departments. The fifth was the landscaping and tree cutters. The sixth was street repairs and signs repair or excavating projects. When there were any problems, Smith would rearrange the work crews so that problems could be solved when they occurred. The DPW office had an emergency overnight crew who could take care of emergencies that occurred after business hours; for example, burst pipes and fallen trees. Finally, there was snow plowing and sanding through the winter to keep the public safe.

During my second week of work, a newly hired worker started. His name was Samuel Jones, and he had grown up and attended school in Butland. Samuel and I got along and become friends. When the guys took a lunch break, we would all have a conversation, and the main topic was Smith, our superintendent. The guys explained how Smith would screw the guys over. I asked what they meant, and Moe Downing said that Mark Batch, the old highway foreman, had been denied the assistant supervisor position because Smith had stopped the promotion. All the guys took turns explaining all the problems Smith had caused over time at the DPW office. Samuel explained that he had gone to school with Smith, and he said that Smith had been a bully as a child. The one person who knew all Smith's stories about damaging the careers of DPW workers was Foreman Scott Craw.

I explained to the guys that I wasn't a pushover; I would argue the issues of any problem I had and then take it to a level of legal arbitration. Moe said that I should to be careful about what I said because the walls had many ears. I asked if he meant snitches. Moe said yes. I told him that Smith had been trying to get me to snitch on the guys. Moe asked what I had said in return. I told him I had told Smith I wouldn't that. Moe said I should be worried about that answer over time because it could come back to bite me.

Meanwhile, days seemed to pass quickly in the piercing cold of November while the guys and I worked collecting the trash and doing other jobs. November 2013 was a very cold month—colder than past Novembers. The garbage was still picked up no matter what kind of weather conditions prevailed. Smith was the constant topic of conversation around break-time and lunchtime because he was holding up the new contract for the association union for the Butland DPW office and workers. Foreman Scott Craw was upset about this. He remembered that

Smith's predecessor, Larry Smalls, would always take care of the workers before anything else. Smith, on the other hand, was there only for himself. Smith would find ways of cutting back the budget and then turn the saving into a raise for himself. That year, his raise was an 80 percent! The workers needed their small raise to support their families. The workers' raise was about 7 percent, which is quite small compared to the boss's 80 percent. These are just a few of the goings on that made all the workers upset with Superintendent Smith.

Scott also explained that I would have started with a higher hourly wage if the new contract had been in place. The new contract had a fiscal year date of July 1. The contract covered a three-year cycle with a specific percent raise each year. Scott said, for example, that a 7 percent raise yearly would break down as 2 percent the first year and second year and then 3 percent the third year. Unfortunately, Smith held up the contract for a long time, hurting the workers and their families financially. These are problems are similar to the problems that happen in towns and cities all over the country. Workers are at the mercy of politics and policies and people who hold public office. The leaders we put in office can't tie their shoes, never mind run an office of power in this country. In so many cases, the public pays taxes for the mistakes and criminal actions made by politicians in public office at all levels of government. All the politicians in this country should be ashamed of their policy making and their conduct with regard to treating the citizens of this country.

The month of December was even more bitter than November. I talked to Samuel about our progress with the town and whether we were doing well or poorly as new workers. Samuel agreed that nobody shared any information about the new workers' quality of work. At the end of the day, we saw Smith. Samuel and I asked Smith how we were working out as new workers—good or bad. Smith replied with a derogatory answer, saying that, as long as trucks were all in by 3:30 in the afternoon, we were doing okay. We asked what he meant, but he just walked away from us, leaving us both looking at each other as we wondered what had just happened.

Shortly after that conversation, the bosses from upstairs came to roll call one morning to pass out the assignments. Foreman Scott said he wanted me to stay with him that day. I asked what we would be doing. Scott said that Smith wanted me to do some carpentry work. He asked me if I did carpentry work, and I told him I did. I asked him if he'd seen my truck that I plowed with. It was full of my tools and toolboxes. And it was equipped a ladder rack to carry the ladders I used for carpentry and construction work. Scott said that the rack could have come with the truck when I bought it. I told him I had ordered the truck that way and I had gone to Yellow Hill Regional High in Banton. It was there I learned carpentry. All this information was on my application when I got hired for the town of Butland. I had been in business since 1980. I said, "Didn't Smith tell you? Have you seen my application?" Scott replied that Smith hadn't said anything about me being a carpenter or a contractor. Scott said that Smith just wanted me to do the work of a carpenter that day. I said I could do that work and much more, including the work required for all construction phases. Scott showed me the carpentry work that had to be done. He explained that the windows in the back of the building were new and needed to be trimmed on the inside and outside. But for now, because it was winter, I was to do only the inside trim. I asked if they had a nail gun I could use, and Scott said no. I told him I had one, and I asked him if I could use it for the work. He said I could because using it would get the work done faster. There was a total of eleven windows to trim out on the inside. I got the work done within four workdays.

On the last day, when I was cleaning up, Smith asked how I was doing. I said I was doing okay, and the window trim was finished. He asked why it had taken me so long to do the work. I was baffled by the question. I told him I had used my own nail gun, which had made things easier and faster. Smith said he had heard that I didn't know carpentry." Once again, I was baffled; I didn't understand why he had said that. I asked him what he was talking about, and I reminded him about my application. I told him I'd been in business since 1980. He asked how he could know I was telling the truth. I told him that, if he needed proof, he could have asked for references when I was interviewed. As Smith turned away, he said, "You are walking on thin ice, Vince." Meanwhile, the guys complimented me on my carpentry. Finally, I saw Scott and explained what had just happened with Smith. Scott said, "Smith is starting with you now?"

During the week before Christmas, I gave a Dunkin' Donuts gift card and a Christmas card to Robert Smith, thanking him for hiring me and helping me over the years when I was plowing for the town of Butland. He thanked me for the cards and asked how I was adjusting to the job. I told him, fine, and I mentioned that it seemed colder that year than other years. Smith said we were going to have a bad winter. I then wished him and his family happy holidays, and proceeded to leave the office. Smith wished me and my family happy holidays, and I thanked him.

CHAPTER 3
The Unthinkable

The celebration of the holiday season was over, and it was now mid January. Rhode Island was starting to get hit with an onslaught of snowstorms between January and February. During this storm season, all of the workers were called in to plow and sand. I was assigned an old utility truck that would be my truck for all the snowstorms. This particular morning, I picked up the keys to my truck and headed out to start it up and clear off the snow. Foreman James Great from the repair shop explained that the truck was old and served as the fuel truck for the equipment. He told me to be careful because the shift sometimes stuck. Moe told me the shift cable needed to be replaced. He said I should get as much use out of the old cable as possible; then he would replace it when it finally broke. Jokingly, I said, "Okay, Moe! We will drive till it breaks!"

I worked all day collecting garbage and then worked all night plowing. All the guys called snow plowing blood money. Working around the clock can take a toll on people. This is why the Motor Vehicle Registry has laws against working and driving all day and night without sleep or rest. But our local governments, tend to overlook these rules when snow plowing is required. This is one of the reasons commercial licenses for trucks are important.

In the coldest of the night air, and sometimes early in the morning, we would often get a call about coming in to sand the roads; preparing the roads for the public to go to work. The department used their sanders during the day when the snow melted or at night when the temperature dropped or for other safety reasons. There were eight main drivers and four alternate drivers. At the beginning of the season, the eight main drivers took all the overtime for themselves. As the season progressed, the eight main drivers had a chance to let an alternate driver fill in on a sanding job at night or in the morning. There were also times the DPW office had only four drivers for sanding.

Act 6:30 in the morning, I was called in from sanding the roads. There were only four drivers sanding. The four of us had to cover the entire town before the citizens took to the roads. But before I could finish my sanding routes, I was called back in. When I got back to the office, I asked why I had been called back. Smith told me I was going to work on the garbage trucks. He said he'd send another worker to finish the streets. I told him he had twelve sanding drivers, and eight of them hadn't shown up when he had called them. I told him they wouldn't be in that day either. I asked why he had called me in when he had no sanding drivers. Throwing trash onto a truck is a laborer's job, and I was qualified to do the sanding job. He reminded me that I was a truck driver and a laborer. I agreed, but I told him that, because he had no other drivers, he shouldn't take me off a sanding job to do a labor job. Lots of workers could fill the labor job. Smith said he heard me, but he still needed me on the trash crew. As I walked away, I was thought about how Smith didn't know how to run his work crews.

When I got to my garbage truck, I asked Moe Downing why Smith would call me in from sanding when the streets were not finished. Moe explained that Smith exhibited favoritism with some of the workers who were his "little pets." I told Moe that Smith had initially wanted me to squeal on the workers with any information he might find useful. Moe asked me how I had responded to that. I explained that I refused because I had been the boss of my own company and would never have done anything like that to my workers. Moe got upset about what I had said about Smith's request. He suggested I tell Scott, the highway foreman, about Smith setting workers against each other. I took his advice. When I explained the facts of the conversation between Smith and I to Scott, he got upset because I was not the first person that Smith had approached with this scheme. Scott explained all the dirty deeds done within the office of the DPW, and especially those done by Robert Smith. The other workers also got upset with the situation because this was not the first time these problems had surfaced.

At the same time, Smith's "little pets" heard about the information I shared with Moe and Scott. Scott said the current issues were the reason Smith stopped a union from coming in and helping the workers. Smith had a lot of influence, and he used threat tactics within our office. Smith degraded the workers in front of the other workers, and he threatened their jobs. He used many different ways of intimidating the workers. Basically, he had free rein over the DPW office, and for him, there were no consequences.

During the second blizzard of a snowstorm, all the workers worked around the clock again. This time, the storm occurred on a weekend. This was helpful for the workers because they would be able to rest before Monday, a workday. Smith drove around during this storm and start degrading the plowing job workers were doing. He did this over the CB radios so everyone could hear. The workers all knew each other's routes. Smith started with my route and degraded my work plowing. I saw him on water street, and Smith saw me coming out of water street with my plow down. He began yelling that Water Street hadn't been plowed, and he demanded that someone had to get over there and clean the street. I picked up my CB radio and said, "Robert, I'm here, and you just saw me plowing. What are you doing? Robert, don't degrade me in front of the workers by saying I'm a bad worker and not doing my job plowing!" Smith would not answer the CB radio.

Some of the workers called me on my cell phone to congratulate me for standing up for myself with Smith; no one had ever done that before. Later, other workers took me aside and said I had done the right thing by standing up for myself. I told my fellow workers that I always speak up for my rights and the people I work with when bosses lie and hide the truth about problems. Scott told me, "You are the kind of boss we need for this office." He told me I was aware of the laws and workers' rights on the job and under other circumstances. I told Scott that supervisors should take care of their workers because the workers make them shine. In return, supervisors should make the workers feel good about their work, and they would shine.

Scott saw me later and explained that Smith wanted to hurt me; the signs were there. Scott said Smith had done this to other people, and there was no recourse. Smith's words were gold to the authorities in the town hall, plus Smith had grown up and lived in Butland his entire life. Even if I was right, Smith would make it wrong for me. I told Scott that I had never conducted business or treated workers the way Smith did. Scott said that Smith was a bully and a liar, a problem waiting to happen. He advised me not to challenge him in any way, including when I was right and he was wrong, especially in front of the other men. I told Scott I had good business values and that personal values are wrong in business.

I have never believed in going along with wrong people, but when I am right, I won't stop either. My tolerance goes from zero to a hundred in seconds, for good or bad. Scott explained that I would lose my job if I were to get physical. I told him I knew that problem, but I wouldn't back down either; I believe I'm a defender, not a fighter, especially with bullies. I hate bullies who take advantage of people and hurt them any way they can. Scott told me to be careful about standing up for myself with Smith and his little snitches. He told me that everything I said was getting back to Smith, and Smith would use it against me in time.

Smith backed off from any confrontation for the time being. The sixth storm came through Rhode Island; it was going to drop about twelve inches of snow. My night of plowing was going pretty well until the shift cable broke. I called James Great and explained that the cable had broken. Moe called Smith with the news. Meanwhile, Moe came out to my location and towed the truck back to the DPW office. When I got back to the office, Smith said, "You broke my truck." I started to laugh and told him he had known the cable was about to break. It was just a matter of time before it finally broke. Smith told me my shift was over because he had no other trucks to drive. I told him I could drive my own truck, but he said I couldn't because the department's insurance policy wouldn't cover my truck. One of the workers came in told Smith that he had to go home because of a family emergency. I saw an opening to drive his truck for the rest of the storm. I ask Smith if I could use that truck. At the time, we were in the office with other office people. Smith asked if I knew how to drive a bigger truck with a clutch. I looked at Smith in disbelief. He knew my experience, and he knew I had a class A commercial driver's license. In my business I had often rented trucks and heavy equipment that required a commercial driver's license.

When Smith asked me if I knew how to drive the "big" truck, I lost it! I was so mad and so embarrassed. I reminded him that he had hired me because I met the requirements of the job, one of which was a commercial driver's trucking license and heavy equipment license. He had read my resume and application. When he hired me, he had praised my potential for the job and told me that I would be a good asset. But he was knowingly trying to make me look incompetent on the job. And he was doing it in front of the workers. I finished by saying, "That is a poor excuse for you being a superintendent."

Smith said, "If you know how to drive a double-stick standard truck, be my guest and go." I told him I'd started driving a double-stick truck back in the 80s. I left the office, jumped into the truck, started it up, and plowed my route. I had no problems with that kind of truck or transmission. I heard later that, when I left the office, Smith had started shooting off his mouth. I had pissed him off with my little speech. No one had ever stood up to Smith. He was just a bully, and that was reinforced when people witnessed the confrontation between Smith and me. I had turned the table on Smith. He had tried to embarrass me, but I had turned it all back to him by telling him the truth.

Dark Justice White Collar Crimes

CHAPTER 4

Spring Time

After a brutal winter, it felt good to feel the fresh air of spring. The ZYX office and workers would start cleaning up from winter into spring. Robert would call me up to his office. Before I went upstairs, the guys would say lookout jokingly for the Vaseline; Robert likes that Vaseline. The meaning would be that Robert would screw you over and stick it into your ass, especially when he is being a prick to you. I went upstairs to Robert's office, knocked on the door, and Robert said to come in, Vince. I asked how was he doing, and Robert said fine. I asked what I could do for him. Robert asked if I had a heavy equipment license.

"Yes, I do."

"Which one do you have?"

"2A heavy equipment license," I responded.

Robert asked, "So, you could run an excavator and all the machines under that classification?" I said yes.

"Do you work for excavating companies?" He asked. I said yes.

"How did they conduct a test with the applicants?"

I told Robert they would have a site with no building around and told the person to get in the machine and start it. Then they would ask the person to do some movements with the machine. Robert asked how the boss would know if applicants could work the machine beside their resume. I told him this is why they had a site set up for new applicants, so they don't destroy anything. They would test all the applicants, machines, and trucks when applying for the position. The people would have to pass a test and simple movements of the machines, then more difficult movements between trees. The same would be for trucks, and they would see if people could back up, uncouple the fifth wheel, shift the transmission, and then do a road test. As a boss with my own company, I would see if the guys would know how to use the saws and nail guns and anything else I needed with tools operations. I then asked why are you asking me these questions? Robert said, "Since you were a boss at one time, I want to see how you would handle the issues of testing the workers. A new position has opened up, and the workers do not have the skills to operate the heavy equipment. There is only a handful that have experience with the machines and trucks with shifting. One of the guys turns the machine over, digging the hole just the other day. Another guy loaded the salt for the sanders and turned that machine over. The workers don't have any experience; you, on the other hand, have worked doing excavating work and running other machines as well. I would like to give you the position, but you haven't been here for a year. Robert would say, "OK, that's all I need to ask about. Thank you." As I walked away to go back to work, I started to think about why Robert didn't have the knowledge to handle the workers and their experience. Once again, Robert doesn't have the knowledge or experience that a superintendent should have in order to run the ZYX office.

A couple of days later, I came in from the garbage route for lunch, washed my hands, and Robert saw me. Robert told me he had some news for me. He said I did not come in when called for sanding. I was baffled. I asked why he asked this question at the end of March after the winter season was over. I told him, the first time I missed sanding, he should have expressed the complaints then and not after months later. Robert would ask, why didn't you come in when called for sanding times? I did come in two times, and then I said I was also not shown how all the trucks operated in the dark and with the sander.

All of the trucks you have are different, plus the fact of being in the dark makes things more complicated. I also don't know all of the routes and streets. Robert then said you were lying and did not want to come in. I said to Robert; no, not true; I guess you don't train the workers with the vehicles or anything else? This is why the workers don't know the vehicles or machinery and have accidents. Robert then walks away, pissed off again because I was right with my information about the job and me being a boss at one time. At this point, I started to think about what Robert was trying to do to me. I then remembered what Scott and the guys explained about Robert being a bully. I would have a hard time thinking negatively about Robert, but with everything that was happening between Robert and me, I had a hard time believing it was happening to me. There was a difficult issue because Robert helped me when I was a subcontractor and an employee. When Robert hired me, he explained that I would be good for the town. Another difficult issue is that Robert is helping people, and on the other hand, Robert is knocking people down. My mind started going in different directions; what would I do with this problem between Robert and me? The problem I had was that I put in 11 years waiting for this job that I had with the town. The job meant so much to me, and Robert hurt my job and career. Robert would destroy my chance with the town and all the time I put into the job. I would need my job for a better future with buying a house, a new truck, and a new marriage.

The ZYX office will start doing repair work and new projects when spring comes. I would work on windows inside the building, putting up new trim over the winter. Scott said I would do the outside trim for the windows when the spring comes. We would come in on a Saturday for overtime. I ask Scott how long of a day working on a Saturday. Scott never replied to my question. Scott said to get the tools and start working on the outside trim. Scott bought some new PVC trim wood boards we would use instead of the pine trim boards. The job would take about two days of working on Saturdays. On the second Saturday, Robert would come in at the end of the day and check out the work. Robert would say hello to me, Scott, and Ben Jokes. Robert would start talking to Scott about the new contract and how the workers were upset with Robert for not signing the contract. Scott would explain that the workers don't have a real union for negotiations or a proper person to represent the workers in the right way of Union rules and laws. The workers know that you are in charge as a superintendent, plus you influence the association union, which means that the workers have no input on the problems and complaints; at this point, why should the workers care about their work or the ZYX office? The workers need a true union to represent them with the contract, wages, and benefits without your influence. All the workers know that you stop the true union from entering the Butland ZYX office. When you have all the workers know the truth about a boss doing the wrong thing for the workers, they all will get an attitude against the boss or whoever gives those types of problems to the workers. The respect will be lost between boss and workers, and then more significant problems can form from these problems as well.

Scott gave excellent advice to Robert with no good results from Robert. After the first conversation with Robert, Robert would discriminate by talking about Todd Williams, one of the black workers, and how Todd would use his color to make headway within the ZYX office. I ask Robert, are you sure that's the truth about Todd? Todd has never acted that way with me or anyone; Todd is a good guy to fellow workers. Robert would get upset again with me saying what I did about Todd being a good guy, and Todd doesn't use his color with this job. Robert didn't like the fact I was standing up for Todd and his rights as a human being, and nobody needs to hear a racial comment about another person, especially from a superintendent. Things would change between Robert and me; Robert would plot revenge against me, plus the fact I knew a superintendent discriminating against another worker named Todd Williams. Scott would just shake his head and be quiet about the whole conversation. Scott couldn't believe how he explained the problems between Robert and the workers, and then Robert does the problem of discriminating with Todd in front of Scott, Vince, and Ben. Finally, Robert would clarify that he would do something wrong with me or my job.

Robert would boast about all the men he hurt on the job and how he cut the budget for the town ZYX office. Then, when the men did not give in to Robert and his corrupt ways, Robert would fire them from the job, or Robert would give them such a hard time that they would quit their careers in the town. Then, when it came to the budget, Robert would cut back with no union taking over, which also allowed Robert to have all the personal input with the association union and workers with dire results for the workers. The association union was made up of all of the workers at the ZYX office who would be elected into the union office leaders for the association union. The office position had five offices within the association union. The first office was president; the second office was vice president; the third office was treasurer; the fourth office was secretary; the fifth office was record keeper.

Robert would sway the association union leaders and the workers because Robert was a bully in his position as a superintendent. When the association union and the workers did not follow Robert's directions, they would have to deal with his evil ways of acting as superintendent. Then the consequences would also be a bigger problem for the workers or leaders by losing their jobs and other types of punishments. Robert would have the ZYX office under his control with no one to question his authority or actions. Robert's actions would happen for many years until the new contract came into play for the year (new contract begins) on July 1, 2013.

The contract would be on a three-year cycle, with the workers receiving a percentage of the current pay from the year before. The workers were upset with Robert because they did not get their raise or a new contract for July 2013. The workers were underpaid for their work, and the surrounding town with proper unions was getting paid about $10.00 more per hour. Robert would also cut the budget for the town and keep the workers underpaid with no appropriate union that would be independent of the ZYX office without Robert's influences and sways in any way, shape, or form. The association union and workers would argue with Robert and town leaders about the conditions with their benefits, wages, and a new contract for 2013. One of the conditions of the old contract was that the ZYX workers could not strike in the town of Butland. The workers had to work at all times with or without a new contract with the town.

When April started, Robert would catch me in passing and state that you are pushing the problems. Another time Robert would say your job is on the line. Robert would just harass me or anyone else as he pleases. The best part of Robert's complaints is I was working the garbage trucks throwing trash all day, and all the workers knew that Robert had it in for me, giving me a hard time. Scott would ask people to work Saturdays, so we could paint inside the building where the new windows were. This wall was about 300 ft long and 15 ft high; we would paint, taking two Saturdays. We would have about six guys to come in and work painting for those Saturdays. Robert would see me about a week later and say that I heard you were complaining about working Saturdays. I said to Robert I don't know what you are talking about, Robert. Why would I complain about working when I ask for overtime? Robert said that I had disappeared for a while as well. Once again, I don't know what you are talking about, Robert. Then I told Robert that everyone knows that you are riding me and giving me a hard time. I said that I am doing my job, and that is it; where you are getting this information, I don't know, but it is wrong information, or it's just a lie from you only. Which one is it, incorrect information or a liar, Robert? Robert would then walk away like he always does. When you challenge a bully, they don't know how to handle or expect the situation that you reverse back to themselves. The only reason Robert would walk away was that I was right all the time. Plus, the fact that Robert was dealing with me being a boss at one time was a threat to him and his job. Plus, the point I knew about the discriminating words said in front of foremen Scott, Ben, and me.

CHAPTER 5
May, June & College

When the month of May came around, the complete workforce of the ZYX office would be in full swing of doing projects outside. We would have truck repairs and maintenance work with the equipment, repair the work in our shop yard and town parking lots, paint the fire hydrants, clean Butland's streets, and a unique project for the town square. Robert would ask Scott to build a box for the old railroad tracks displayed in the town square. Robert would say to Scott have Vince help you make the box and install the box in the town square. The day came when a group of workers would go to the town square and dig the hole for this box for railroad tracks. Scott said I would excavate the hole with the excavator, and you and the guys would level the dirt and lay the concrete blocks to support the box. At that time, Robert would show up at the town square and walk around. I was in the hole leveling the blocks with a level. Robert would see me on my knees doing my job leveling the blocks. Robert said, Vince, it looks like you know what you are doing in the hole, then walked away. Then all of a sudden, Robert started yelling at Scott about the box. Robert said what are you doing, Scott? Robert said this is not what I wanted. Scott said you gave me verbal directions, and I followed them. That is not my direction; otherwise, you are a carpenter; you should know your job, Scott. Scott said if you gave better instructions on paper, then I would do a better job for you; I don't know what's inside your mind unless you put it on paper. Scott said Robert; you don't know how to instruct the workers or plan for the project jobs. Robert said that's why I depend on you and other workers and the supervisors to know their work and job and get it done. One of the reasons I give Vince a hard time with his work around the yard. Scott said, no, you were just harassing Vince over nothing he did wrong and lying about your story about Vince. When I saw how Robert disrespected Scott in the town square and then said something about me simultaneously, I knew things would worsen for me and anybody who would help me with the problem. In all of my work life, I have never seen a superintendent yell at a foreman in public or in front of other workers or the public. It was unheard of, yelling on the job and embarrassing for the workers and foreman, plus the superintendent that is doing the yelling and embarrassing himself. Robert was a man with a high position in the town as a superintendent. Still, this man was an incompetent man with no knowledge of the work or his position as a superintendent, especially when Robert moved up in the ZYX office from a young man. When I saw that Robert didn't know the work, I couldn't believe that this man had his position; I have more experience than Robert as an owner, boss, and worker of my own business.

At the end of May, the town had a program with college students to give them a job for the summer with the ZYX office. The college program was a great situation for the students, and it gave them a chance for the students to earn money for the summertime and learn about work and job experience. The college students were good kids learning a new job from the ZYX office. The ZYX office would pair one student with a town employee and driver for the garbage trucks. The college students would be here from May to the end of August when they would go back to school. The students would receive minimum wage pay working at the ZYX office. One of the students was a son of a friend from my school time. My friend's son's name was Chris Baralucci; we would talk about his dad and family members as we threw trash all day. Robert also explains to the workers to look out for the college students. I would work with all the college students and have a good friendship. When June came around, Robert would start picking on the college students. Robert would complain about how the college students would call out sick and any minor thing that the college student did wrong. When Robert complained about the college kids, this would take some pressure off me being bullied by Robert. At the same time, it wasn't fair for the college students to receive any problems from Superintendent Robert. One of the college student's families made plans to go on vacation just before college started in September. Mike was a college student asking for advice from full-time employees if he should tell Robert about the vacation time in August. The workers would say yes, it's the proper thing to do so Robert can make other plans when you leave for your vacation. You are also giving him a month and a half in advance to make any changes. When Mike saw Robert the next morning at roll call, Mike explained that his family had made plans for a vacation at the end of August. Robert got so upset with Mike that Robert said you have two choices. The first choice is to stay and work till you leave for college, or the second choice is to go on vacation, and I fired you. Mike was so upset for doing the right thing explaining his family vacation and yet losing his job over a bully. Mike said to Robert take your job and shove it up your ass; I quit. When Mike came into the lunchroom, Mike explained what happened to Robert and the choices Robert had made. Once again, all the guys said that we were sorry about Superintendent Robert. But, don't worry, have fun for the summer and your vacation. Robert would say later that he had to make an example of the student because of all the students calling out sick. All the workers would be upset, but nobody was going to challenge Robert and lose their jobs.

Robert would return to me with a vengeance for other problems around the office. Robert would punish me by keeping me on the garbage trucks with the college students all summer. When the college students are there in the summer, it gives the workers a chance to do other projects and a break from the garbage trucks. Robert thought he could punish me, but when he heard that I like working the garbage trucks, he was upset with the news from his little snitches. Robert thought he could run me down with the college students, but I threw the trash and ran to the next stop of trash barrels. Robert would get that message and was even more piss-off. The difference between co-workers and college students is about 20-40 years in age, and the speed of a younger person throwing the trash compared to an older person throwing the trash. Some of the employees were up in age, getting ready for retirement, whereas you have a 20-year-old with energy. Many of the workers would have a hard time with the speed of summertime heat and the college students. Meanwhile, I had no problem keeping up with the summertime heat or the college students. Summertime is a good time for me to accelerate for me and work. The college students and I would run from trash barrel to trash barrel. The truck would be slower than us because it had to move slowly for safety reasons. The beginning of the summer was looking good, especially when I was away from Robert.

Once the college students got to know the routine of the garbage routes, the speed of doing the route got faster. It would take longer to do the routes in the wintertime because of cold, snow, ice, and more trash because of the holidays. Summertime was more manageable because people would go on vacations, and people would be out more in the summertime. The workers worked too fast with the college kids, and Robert complained about coming into the yard too early. The schedule for winter was 7.00 am to about 2.30 pm, and the summertime was 7.00 to 1.30 pm, if not sooner than that. It got to the point of the garbage trucks were finding a place to hide from the office and Robert. Part of the reason we were hiding is that when we returned to the office, there would not be any work for us to do, and the office didn't want people hanging around the office waiting for 3.30 pm to go home. The bad thing about the garbage crew hiding is that it would take time to get back to the office if we were needed for other work. Summertime was a good time for all the workers because of vacation time, July 4th, beach time, and having fun in the sun.

The month of June came, which would be a sad time for me. I had a great aunt that was in a nursing home. My aunt was my grandmother's sister, and she lived till 103 years old. When the doctors explained to the family that her time was coming, I relayed the message to my job that I would have a funeral coming up and need time off. Robert would ask how much time I said I didn't know; my aunt was like a 2nd mother to me, and I didn't know how to handle the emotions. I'm not too good with people passing away, especially when we are a close family. Robert would say that your work is just as important, and you are pushing your job aside. I said that I was giving you well enough notice of a funeral coming to my family and me and that this woman was like a second mother to me. Robert said I need workers to do their jobs without excuses. I said this isn't about me; this is about family, obligations, and respect for the deceased. Then I said, I'm just giving a notice; of a funeral for my aunt. And when this may happen to her? When she does pass away, are you going to fire me or give me more problems on the job? Robert then said that's why you are on the garbage trucks forever. I told him fine because I do my job all day, then go home without seeing you or hearing from you, and no complaints, Robert.

CHAPTER 6
July, August & Job Ending

The day came when my aunt passed away, and I called into work to explain that I would need from Wednesday to Sunday off, and I'll be in on Monday. Robert would ask the workers if Vince's aunt had passed away. One of the workers said I know of the family, and yes, the aunt did pass away; here are the obituaries in the newspaper. Another worker overheard Robert saying to the office secretary; I was hoping that Vince was lying about the aunt passing away. Robert said I would use his lies against him and then fired him. Robert would try to find excuses to fire me; Robert was determined to fire me for no reason other than his insecurities and ignorance. Robert would take time and chase me around, looking for an excuse to fire me from my job. Robert would ask his little pets to report any information about Vince, whether or not it's good or bad. The conditions would happen all of July by the end of July; I could not take the hostile conditions that Robert was creating. The workers try to explain to Robert not to abuse, bully, and harass Vince; Vince is a good worker and a good guy. Robert ignores the worker's explanation to stop abusing, bullying, and harassing Vince.

On August 1, 2014, I started to feel sick with my stomach receiving pains and cramps. It would happen for two weeks with pain, cramps, and final diarrhea. August 15 was a Friday after work; I ran to the bathroom and sat for hours on the toilet in pain and diarrhea. The problem would happen all weekend long with the symptoms and problems; I decided Monday I would call in sick and go to the doctor. On August 18, Monday, I called into work and explained that I was ill with diarrhea and going to the doctor's office. The secretary said to Vince, don't forget a doctor's note explaining the problems you have with the job and for Robert. The secretary said that Robert was looking for a reason to fire you from your job. I said I knew I would get the letter from the doctor. I said to the secretary thank you for looking out for me; it's nice to have good friends to help me when you have a boss trying to destroy me.

I would go to the doctor's office, and the doctor would run some tests to see if there was a physical problem. When the doctor received the tests, there was nothing wrong. The doctor looked at my medical records and said I have IBS (irritable bowel syndrome) and medical problems. The doctor asks me if I've been under stress conditions. I said yes to my job, and a superintendent was giving me a hard time and threatening my job. The doctor said I would give you a letter to excuse you from work for a week; I also want to see you before returning to work. I would go by the office and pass my doctor's letter, excusing me from work. One week later, I saw the doctor, and the doctor ran some more tests to see if anything changed with the tests. The tests came back with no problems on a physical level, and the doctor said I want you to see a psychiatrist and see if they can explain any stress problems. I will give you a letter for another week to excuse you from your job. I passed in the first letter on August 18 after the doctor visits with no problems. With the second letter when I passed the note to secretary Wendy Potts, who was acting boss for the day.

I started to get sick with pains in the chest, head-spinning, hard time breathing, feeling weak, and shaking feelings. Wendy said to go home and take care of myself. When I got home, I ran to the bathroom and died in pain with IBS cramps and diarrhea on the toilet. When I get diarrhea, it drains me of all my energy, and running back and forth to the bathroom; eventually, I start bleeding from diarrhea when I am wiping myself. I also began to think about what would happen when I talked to Wendy, and I concluded that I was having an anxiety attack with Wendy and explaining my health conditions to her. The next day I called the doctor's office and left a message with the doctor's secretary; I believed I had an anxiety attack yesterday. Can I see the doctor? The doctor would call me hours later and say that I needed to see a psychiatrist to help, and they would help me with anxiety attacks. The doctor left me baffled and hanging when I looked for medical help. It was like she was pushing off her responsibilities as a doctor.

I would set up an appointment with the psychiatrist, and within the week of the doctor's letter excusing me from work, I saw the psychiatrist. The psychiatrist was Dr. Vera Smits, and she would ask what the problems you were having were. First, I explained that I was having problems with IBS, and then I was having anxiety problems related to stress from my boss bullying me and threatening my job. My Primary Doctor, Lori Iceberg, said that I have stress-related problems from my work conditions. Dr. Smits explains that I can give you medication for your problems, and you need to seek therapy for your problems. However, if you gave me medications, it would interfere with my job when I return to work. Dr. Smits said I know that, but it is also your job doing the damage to you. Dr. Smits said that I would give you a note to excuse you from work for a week, and then your new therapist will help you from that point going forward with your job. So, I would make another appointment with a therapist within the week of Dr. Smits's letter.

I got the letter from the doctor and called my daughter to have her turn in the letter for me to my job. When my daughter Jenny got to the ZYX office, she saw Wendy and gave her the letter from the doctor. Wendy said I would have to call Robert and say that Vince was passing in a third doctor's note to excuse him from work. Robert would be yelling over the phone, saying that I was dismissed from my job at the ZYX office. Wendy asked Robert do you want the letter? Robert said no, I don't need the letter. Vince is gone from this job. My daughter couldn't believe that a superintendent boss would act meanly about a man or a man's illness. Otherwise, my father's boss caused and is the one who gave him health problems that are being addressed from a doctor's office. Plus, Robert would refuse and not receive an excuse letter from the doctor. Jenny would leave the ZYX office upset with this man, Robert, whom she didn't know, but he was acting like a jerk above and beyond belief because of a sick man and then rejected the doctor's letter. Jenny would come home and tell me what happened with Wendy and Robert.

While my daughter was on her way home, Robert would make a call on my cell phone. Robert would start yelling at me over the phone by saying you are an asshole for going to the doctors and using them as an excuse for working. I was trying to explain to Robert (with the anxiety starting up and getting a very strong reaction) that I wasn't lying about anything. I have problems because of you and how you have attacked me in so many different ways over this job with your insecurity, incompetence, and ignorance. You don't deserve this position as a superintendent, and you don't know how to handle the workers or jobs. You have been faking your job all this time and your life. Robert said that you are dismissed from your job, Vince. I said you couldn't do that because this job is related to stress problems of a job and boss with malicious intention from a superintendent boss; all this is because of you and the stress you have given me as a worker due to stress from you

Robert. Robert would hang up the phone to end the conversation. My daughter would walk in at that time and explain what happened in the ZYX office. Jenny would say you need to file complaints against Robert and the town of Butland that they are both responsible for the way you are sick. Robert would go around the ZYX office and boast that he got Vince dismissed from his job. The workers wanted to say something to Robert about Vince's issue, but if they did, it was a question if they wished to keep their jobs and didn't act against Robert or the town. The workers had to put it away and forget about it or lose their jobs.

Dark Justice White Collar Crimes

CHAPTER 7
Finding an Attorney

I was kicked to the curb by a man who destroyed my career as a ZYX worker and injured me with stress-related issues, causing financial ruin and a loss of everything that would lead me to have a normal life in our world. Now comes the task of looking for an attorney to handle my case and legal problems. The first question asked by an attorney is what are the physical problems you have. When you explain to an attorney how a superintendent boss can stress me out on the job and discriminate against black people, bully me, harassment to me, swear, name-calling, and many other things. The answers you received from an attorney are very cruel. The attorneys who handle stress or related mental cases like mine would make unbelievable excuses for why they wouldn't take the case upon themselves. Some of the attorneys would answer how much money you have to spend. When you find attorneys who will take the time to hear the case from you, you run into a mental illness problem that is hard to prove. Then I replied that witnesses could prove the truth of job abuse of mental health from a superintendent boss. The attorneys would say no worker will put their job on the line and get fired for helping you, and they lose their job. Trying to find an attorney would be very difficult in Rhode Island.

I would try all types of sources to find an attorney with very little luck. Finally, I would file online to find an attorney, and one attorney did answer the file online. His name was Attorney Bob Keyhole, and he would call my cell phone and ask what kind of discrimination. I said racial discrimination, age, and health. Bob explains that you need to file before the board of discrimination, and you would only have one year to file these papers from the time of the incident. You would also need to have $3,000.00 for me to handle this case. So, at the end of September, I would hire Attorney Bob Keyhole, give him $3,000.00, and, in a week or so, Attorney Bob would send an e-mail letter from the town explaining that I was dismissed from my job in the town of Butland. Bob would clarify that this was their way of acting against the facts of you hiring an attorney to dispute your accusation against Superintendent Robert Smith and the town of Butland. Bob would say that this is the official way of telling you don't have a job with the town anymore.

I would e-mail back to Bob saying that I was seeing a doctor to find out what was wrong with my health, and then, in the process, they would dismiss me from my job. At this point, I believe that the town discriminated against me with my health problems and the wrongful dismissal of my job. I also said that if they were smart, to wait until I returned to work and then dismissed me from my job and not before. Bob never got back to me about my e-mail at this point. About a month later, Bob got a settlement offer for $5,000.00 and gave me a call to talk about the settlement. When I heard about the settlement from Bob, I was confused about the proposal, and Bob was pushing the settlement offer. I said to Bob why am I going to accept this offer? I just gave you $3,000.00, and you are going to make money, and I get only the money I gave you in return. I said you haven't even seen the medical bills or the doctors' reports. What are you doing for me? I'm seeing all types of doctors, and you are trying to settle the case? I said you didn't even interview me for my explanation of what my story is and my complaints. What kind of an attorney are you? At the same time, I am dealing with all of the symptoms of anxiety, IBS problems, and stress-related problems. Bob would say I'll get back to you with a better answer. I would never hear that follow-up phone call from Bob.

As time went on, I noticed I was in pain throughout my body, and I couldn't figure out why I was hurting as much as I was. So I would make a doctor's appointment to find out why I felt this way. The doctor asked how I was feeling, and I explained the pain running throughout my body. The doctor gave me a medical paper and asked me to read it, so I did, and the doctor asked how many symptoms I had; according to the article, I said all. The doctor said that you have fibromyalgia, IBS, anxiety, and stress-related issues and problems. They all connect, and that's not good for a human body; I said, agreed, my body seems like it wants to explode from the inside; the doctor said, I'm sure of that. The doctor asked me are you seeing a therapist; I said yes, are you on medicine? I said yes. Well, it's going to take time to heal yourself; I said that it would be a long road with an attorney not doing his job correctly and a town that's lying about my job and related legal problems. The doctor also said that you could correct this problem within three years; after that, the fibromyalgia will be permanent for the rest of your life, with conditions getting worse as time goes on.

Bob would contact me, explaining that the town made the same offer again. Are you willing to accept this offer? I said, no, have you talked to any of my doctors and received any reports from the doctors? Bob would just avoid the question that I ask. I said to Bob that I was just at the doctor's office, and the doctor had just diagnosed me with fibromyalgia and all stress-related illnesses. Once again, Bob, have you asked for any information about my medical information or records? One of the best things that I did was to start keeping records and recording; I also witnessed all these problems from the beginning, when I saw the attorney Bob, and went to doctors' visits. The laws state that recording people is against the laws, but how do you protect yourself when you have professional people taking advantage of people? People who have complaints against a person or town caused my mental stress illnesses; (caused by Robert Smith and the town of Butland). A person like me doesn't have many choices when professional people act in such a way of breaking the laws of this country. I would have two options: to follow the laws of this country or violate the laws of this country. How can I protect my well-being and health from liars and prove the truth to these professional people and authorities people? The problem is that when you have professional people breaking the laws do you follow their examples, or do you do the right thing with the laws you know and uphold the laws for the better? Sometimes a good person has to bend the laws, as the attorneys say, without breaking the laws. It's a sad day in this country, state, and town when professional people and rich people can get away with violating the laws, and the innocent pay the price and lose everything that they have in this world. I would not be protected from lies and deceivers, especially when diagnosed with stress and mental illness. Mental stress illness is an illness that relates to the brain area or related issues. Trust issues would be another problem that would enter my life as a professional person taking advantage of altering the original complaints and avoiding medical and legal records.

I would go back and forth between my attorney Bob and my primary doctor Lori Iceberg; I was trying to get my medical records between them and was receiving no cooperation from either one. Attorney Bob didn't request the records from my primary doctor Lori, and a primary doctor wouldn't cooperate with attorney Bob or me. Doctor Lori did not give the medical records. These problems only increased my fibromyalgia symptoms, IBS, and stress-related problems. The doctors' complications would also increase the distrust factor; I didn't trust anyone, including attorney Bob. Time would pass with no medical records for the attorney Bob. Dr. Lori wasn't cooperating with attorney Bob. Attorney Bob and my girlfriend Lisa Warren went to a discrimination board hearing without any medical records. Plus, attorney Bob's version of his lies with his complaint. Compared to my actual original complaints of what I explained and experienced to Bob about the discrimination and other problems. The bottom line with my criticisms of the discrimination was not my original complaints. Still, the complaint was from the attorney Bob's version, and the actual version was lost and covered up by attorney Bob.

On the day of the discrimination hearing, attorney Bob wasn't even prepared for the hearing; attorney Bob only had one copy of the complaints papers. Attorney Bob needed four copies. One was for me, one was for the town, one was for himself, and one for the hearing judge. When I read the papers, I said this isn't how I explain the information and complaints to you in your office. Attorney Bob would say to be quiet and just sit there. Then, the introductions would commence in the hearing room, with my girlfriend sitting in the back of the room. The town attorney Gram Stoneman started with complaints about my attorney Bob not being prepared for the hearing and that his complaint wasn't adequately prepared for the judge. The judge didn't even address that issue and asked about attorney Bob's complaints.

Attorney Bob would answer racial, age, and health discrimination from Superintendent Robert Smith with the town of Butland. Then the judge would ask the town attorney, Gram, about the town's disposition on this matter. Attorney Gram would explain that Superintendent Robert Smith did nothing racial or with age or health problems, and the town denies all allegations. Finally, the judge asks Mr. D'Angelo whether he can explain the facts of his case and his side of the story. That's when anxiety hit me, and I tried to explain the complaints as I was trembling, my voice was broken up, and my head was spinning and getting dizzy. I explain how Robert's racial discrimination happened by talking about another worker named Todd, a black man, and my friend. The judge asked how this interferes with you, and I said that I was involved with a woman of Black American and Indian American descent and other ancestry descent. I also have other family members with interracial relationships. I considered any insults with racial comments offensive beyond belief and outright ignorance of the human race.

The judge asks whether the town has anything to say on this matter. Attorney Gram said we sympathize with Mr. D'Angelo and his family matters; Robert said nothing related to those conditions of racial comments. Meanwhile, attorney Bob just sat there doing nothing for this argument or the case. It looked like I was alone representing myself without an attorney, even though he sat right beside me. The judge then said OK and asked what the issue was about the age problem, Mr. D'Angelo. Robert expected the older workers to work as hard as a college student in his early 20s. We would have college students that the town hires for the summertime. I know this is a form of discrimination by age. Men aged 20 to 40 years and older work hard but never can compare to 20 years old speed and energy. Robert also explains that he prefers the more senior men because they have family and bills to keep them working, unlike the 20-year-olds as no responsibilities and do show up for work and call out all the time.

Robert would put young against old with everything meaning age, work standards, etc. The judge then said OK, now what about your health problems I said that I was getting sick and went to the doctor to find out what was wrong with me, and the next thing I knew was that Robert was dismissing me from my job. It leads us to believe that Robert didn't even acknowledge my health as being sick on the job. The judge said I would take the information and investigate the allegations; in this case, I will notify the attorneys when I have a decision. The hearing was adjourned, and my girlfriend Lisa and my attorney Bob left the office, I started to ask questions about the procedures of what happened. I told Bob that you weren't even prepared for the hearing, and you changed my original complaints and problems. We have two separate complaints at this hearing, Bob. I said, One complaint was written from you, and another complaint from me verbally? That you didn't even take notes on with the case. Do you think that will win? I asked if there was any way to correct this hearing, Bob. Bob said no, once the complaints and hearing are made, that's it for you. So that means that I lost the hearing; Bob said that's not true; you can win the hearing. I asked what would happen now. Attorney Bob said It would take up to two years for an answer. I said OK, but are we going to file complaints with the courts.

Attorney Bob would avoid the question in front of my girlfriend Lisa and me. Attorney Bob would give excuses about the whole situation. The anxiety was running high now; I exploded at attorney Bob and said you would provide me with a straight answer. Attorney Bob said no, I would not file court documents for the case. I asked why; attorney Bob just walked away, leaving me standing there with my girlfriend, Lisa. Lisa would say you need to find a better attorney, especially when he walks away and quits the case. I had no choice; I wanted this to go to a courtroom and be adequately heard and legally justified. The problem is to find another attorney to accept this case and do the job the right way.

When I got home to the family, Lisa and I would explain how everything happened with the attorney and how attorney Bob just stole my money and ran away in front of Lisa and me.

CHAPTER 8
Second Attorney

I needed to find a new attorney since attorney Bob had left me high and dry at the discrimination board office with Lisa and me. Finding an attorney will be more challenging since the first attorney may have made mistakes with the discrimination board. The task of finding a new attorney will take some time. The hearing date was in June of 2015, and by December, I had found a new attorney Allen Moakley. Attorney Allen would ask for a retainer of $5,000.00 to be received before the meeting date. Attorney Allen set up an appointment for February 8, 2016, for an interview about the case and my explanation of my complaints about Robert Smith, my job, and the town of Butland. We would have a second meeting as an interview time, four hours with only interviewing time.

I asked Attorney Allen about our procedures going forward in the case and court procedures. Attorney Allen explains that we will file papers with the courts; one filing will be with workmen's comp. Office in Sealand, RI.

The other filing will be in the superior court in Wedham, RI. I asked about the discrimination board. Attorney Allen said we just have to wait for an answer from them. I explained to Allen that attorney Bob made many mistakes at the discrimination board. Can we file a complaint against the case information that was wrong by attorney Bob and town attorney Gram along with the town? Attorney Allen said no. I want to know and acknowledge the reasons why attorney Bob was lying with his paperwork and complaints. For the judge to be aware of these problems from attorney Bob, attorney Allen said no again. The town of Butland and attorney Gram presented a letter from Scott Craw. He is the highway foreman for the town of Butland. The supposedly written letter by Scott was filled with all lies within this letter. Plus, this letter was written one year later, from the date of the problems, and the foreman didn't sign the letter entered in the records. Attorney Allen said no, there is nothing you or I can do about this problem with discrimination records. The town of Butland and the town attorney, Gram, fouled the case and got away with lying and not telling the correct information to the court of law.

My health problems were only getting worse in time, and dealing with more issues with doctors and attorneys and the town fighting the problems they created. I had a more challenging time with problems of anxiety and stress than nobody could imagine. The issues of fighting my mind and how the body would react; would be very challenging, and dealing with people would only cause more mental and physical stress issues. First, I had to deal with chest pains, confusion, panic attacks, and headaches, and there were only anxiety issues. Then, add in the fibromyalgia issues with the complete body pains and then the IBS issues of diarrhea and running to the bathroom; all of this was stress-related. The rheumatologist doctor said that I would only have up to 3 years to change my fibromyalgia outcome. After that, it will be permanent; the doctor also said that if I were under any more stress over a long period, the fibromyalgia would be permanent and worse with time.

When I hired attorney Allen, Allen explained that he would retrieve all the records from attorney Bob so he could be updated on what he did with the case interviews with Allen and me. I said that would be fine. Within a week of attorney Allen retrieving my records from attorney Bob, I would receive a phone call from attorney Bob. Attorney Bob would ask why you are leaving me and hiring a new attorney for the case. I said for starters, you walked away from me in Sealand; I haven't heard from you for about eight months; you also told me that you weren't going to file in the courts, so what am I supposed to think or do? Attorney Bob said what can I do for you at this point so we can continue an attorney and client relationship. I said are you going to take the case to court? Attorney Bob hesitated with an answer, and I said no, I had already hired an attorney who would take the case to court. Then attorney Bob would start begging me to stay on the case, and I said no, we are all done, and I hung up the phone. I would talk to my mother my family members, and Attorney Allen about the phone call with Attorney Bob. We would all agree that something was weird with that phone call and how he acted. I said that conversions are going on without our knowledge from the town officials, including the town attorney, or maybe more people. My family members would say you'll never know the truth to that answer, and I said yes, I will someday; not sure when but I will find out. Attorney Allen would say it's a possibility; I asked Attorney Allen how the conversation was with Attorney Bob; Attorney Allen said the conversation was okay, and he sent the records. I would only think about some kind of side deal that was going on with the town or town attorney and attorney Bob.

Attorney Allen would ask me to talk to the doctors and see how they would react to a Workmen Comp. case and discrimination case with their cooperation. I explained that attorney Bob didn't even talk to the doctors and get my records. But I did ask the doctors about attorney Bob, and the doctors didn't even know about attorney Bob. Attorney Allen said it'd been two years since the health issues started, and you have only got worse with your health and stress problems. I said that is true, and the doctors haven't cooperated with me; Allen said that might be a problem for the cases because without the doctors explaining your problems to a judge, you don't have a chance and case. I said that there must be a way for the doctors to be obligated to cooperate, or we go around these legal problems. Attorney Allen said we would work on these problems, but for now, you need to try to have the doctors work with us; first, I said OK. Attorney Allen would also say you should apply to social security for benefits; I asked why and Attorney Allen said that if you win SSI, that will make the case harder on the town and attorneys, and you would prove that you are injured from your job. Attorney Allen would come out strong with the correct answer initially, but would the results stay the same until the cases end?

Attorney Allen asked for a list of all my doctors, including my primary Dr. Lori Iceberg, rheumatologist Dr. Peter Orlando, gastrologist Kenneth Sole, neurological Dr. Moel Hatcher, Ph.D. psychiatrist Dr. Jen Chow, therapist Fay Pain, hospital good medical, therapist hospital humans. These people and hospitals needed a signed release of my medical records for attorney Allen to receive medical information for my case. Attorney Allen would request these medical records for our case and an explanation of my medical issues and problems. Attorney Allen would also start asking questions about your need to claim the lawsuits on your taxes; I said what are you talking about, Allen? I said lawsuits never paid taxes. Allen would also say that if we get to a settlement, for example, if the case settles for a million, you will only receive half of the money, in accordance with the courts and laws of this country. Once again, I told Allen this is bullshit what you are telling me. No way is any of this truth about how you are explaining these issues. Meanwhile, my medical issues started to act up and bother me with pain and other issues. I would look into the questions and find out that Allen was lying about what he explained to me about the laws and paying back with taxes and half settlements.

I would start noticing how people were treating me and find out that people were taking advantage of me with my mental stress problems, knowing that I was on medications and going through all of these problems with the medicines. In accordance with the laws of this country, some laws prevent people from taking advantage of disabled people or people with medical conditions. The problems would relate to all the professional people (doctors and attorneys) involved with my cases. These problems would only bring out more reasons for not believing in the people or laws or anything in this world. Robert would start the problems with the job and take advantage of a good worker who had no problems. I started with no health problems, and now I have many health problems; when I started the job, I also with years of working well before I was hired as an employee. Then having the same issues repeated to doctors and attorneys with them taking advantage of me under such medical conditions only worsened things for me and my health and all of the problems involved with the cases. I would also notice that Attorney Allen would give the correct information and then change or avoid the words and the whole story with more problems. Attorney Allen was only trying to confuse the cases more. When I asked Allen about things he said, I noticed attorney Allen would talk in circles with no solution to any questions or answers. These problems would also happen with the doctors involved, and my cases never got the right questions or answers from my doctors, medical health, or records. These problems would only bring out more questions on what is going on with all these professional people that I can't even have an answer about my conditions of medical or legal matters.

I would go to my doctors' appointments and therapy appointments. When I went to the appointments, I tried to explain to the doctors the conditions of my body and what I go through regularly. There are different pains that I go through that are unbelievable; some of the pain is like an aching pain, another pain is a stabbing pain, with this pain feels like a knife or needles going through my body parts, headaches are another type of multiple pains as well. These pains and other conditions would only worsen in time from how the doctors didn't or were unwilling to explain these problems to me. The doctors would explain some things to me, but I feel they never explained all the details or problems or issues they were holding out on the truth of medical issues, problems, and information. One of those issues is fibromyalgia; this is where the most pain originates from and will continue for a lifetime. All of my conditions were stress-related; the main issues were stress that would lead to fibromyalgia and then IBS, then the effects of pain and other issues from stress, anxiety, fibromyalgia, and IBS. I would also explain to the doctors that in just two years, when these issues started, it had only gotten worse and what would be my future with all the pain and medical problems. The doctors would begin to avoid any questions about my medical problems. When I explained that I had an attorney on the cases and that I would need all the doctor's cooperation, the doctors would only avoid the conversation, and no response from the doctors on any answers for me. I would be left hanging again but now with the doctors with no cooperation from them.

I would contact attorney Allen, and I explained that the doctors don't even want to help me with my stress, fibromyalgia, and IBS problems. I had visits with all of them and got no response from them to help me. I said to Attorney Allen that I need to send a letter to introduce myself and with you representing me with my cases. Attorney Allen would say I will send letters to all of your doctors. I will find out that attorney Allen did not send any letters of introduction to all the doctors. He only asked for the medical records from primary and rheumatologist doctors. The doctors didn't even know that attorney Allen had asked for my medical records. I would only find out over time about all of the problems and people involved with my case. I would intentionally watch over everyone who was mishandling, or falsifying information, medical records, legal records, and many other circumstances with my cases.

Personal thoughts: thinking to myself about the problems and what I was going through with all of these professional people, a job that I worked for about 12 years overall, and one man (Robert) who destroyed my future in so many ways that it was difficult to understand on all levels. Then to went to doctors and explained that these stress-related problems are from a job and a superintendent boss Robert Smith and the town of Butland. The doctors avoided my explanations and reasons about the job and my boss on how things happened to me. I got involved with attorney Bob, and he did not represent me or the case right at all; then, I found and hired a second attorney Allen, and Allen started to play the same games as attorney Bob. The attorneys and doctors were only there for money reasons, not justice or medical care. Meanwhile, I was trying to deal with my stress, anxiety, fibromyalgia, IBS, and other conditions. I thought I would lose my mind with all that was happening in my life, and nobody wanted to help or care to help me in any way, shape, or form.

CHAPTER 9
The Letter

Attorney Allen and I received an envelope of papers from the law firm of B.- F.- Y. for the discrimination side of the case against the town of Butland. Law firm B.- F.- Y. sent two copies, one for me and one to attorney Allen. Both of us would go through the paperwork and discover information that was despicable with lies upon lies from my thoughts and how I knew the truth. Attorney Allen started to question and doubt if he should quit the cases at this point. I would call attorney Allen; I explained that I received an envelope and there was a lot of disturbing information about me and the lies from the town with these papers. Attorney Allen said I got the same paperwork, and then attorney Allen said that I agreed there was disturbing information about the case. We need to set an appointment and talk about the new problems and their offer to end this case.

On the appointment day, myself, a family member, and Attorney Allen greeted each other. Then we started to go over the papers. Attorney Allen asked me, what is this Scott's letter about you and your working ability? I explained that this letter was all lies, and I don't think Scott wrote this letter, but this was the same letter they used in the discrimination board hearing that I told you about Allen. I said I think this is a way of them discouraging you with the cases. I have worked for the town for a long time, and I know that Robert and the town would lie about anything in their favor, no matter what the cost would be. I said that the offices (ZYX AND TOWN HALL) don't even keep good records that I saw physically. I said that is why I don't believe Scott wrote the letter to start. I also saw a worker get fired because he asked about his hours for the week and sick time accumulation. I also said that Robert was also suspended from his position as a superintendent for a significant problem. Attorney Allen said that Robert's history doesn't matter; this is only about you. I said, Attorney Allen, this is also about Robert and the dirty ways involved with me and these cases.

Another time is when Robert put pressure on the workers to get rid of the new union that was coming in and was only there a one month. I explained that Robert broke federal laws to stop a Union from entering the ZYX office. Once again, the workers as witnesses to how fast Robert preys on the workers and anything else that gets in his way. Attorney Allen said that you are the issue once again, not Robert. I then said, " Well, I believe that Robert wrote this letter, and these reports about not coming in and sanding the roads are lies about me and my work habits.

Attorney Allen said this issue about you missing sanding dates. Can you explain that story to me? I explained that there are eight main drivers for sanding, and then there are four drivers that are alternates. I went in 2 times and missed four times when they called me. I also said that the ZYX office doesn't show you or teach you anything about our jobs. One of those jobs was sanding and the routes of sanding. I was still learning the streets of Butland. I explained that when Robert brought up this sanding issue, we were in the middle of March and that Robert should have told me the day after the time of sanding and not months later. Attorney Allen would have no advice or response to my statement. I showed Attorney Allen the copies of how the ZYX office and Robert kept their records on scrap paper. They would write on a concrete company pad of paper that I didn't show up when called, but where are the names of other workers who didn't show up either? Once again, no response from attorney Allen. Attorney Allen didn't make good points or that I was wrong with my questions. It was like the question just disappeared into the air. I repeated the questions and got no response from Allen.

Then I would go back to Scott's letter, and I said if Scott wrote this letter, why didn't he sign this letter? Attorney Allen said I don't know. I told Attorney Allen that you should look into this because we would show the truth or lies that the town and Robert are doing to this case and other problems in this ZYX office. Attorney Allen would avoid this issue altogether, and now I started to get upset with Attorney Allen. I would start noticing that attorney Allen wasn't representing me as an attorney would in the proper ways. I would be stuck with an attorney who wasn't correctly working for me, and what was I going to do? I would turn to my family members and ask them if they could advise me in the right direction. I would get answers by talking to another attorney and see what they would do or say about the problems. The attorney would explain that you need to document all the problems from start to finish. I have been doing this from the beginning; that's why I have family members with me on visits with doctors and attorneys so that it's not just my words of he said, and she said problems. Here is another time I would feel like throwing in the towel and giving up. But I would remember what my dad would say to me as a kid never give up when you are right with your problems. My dad would say you need to fight hard to prove that you are right about your problems.

Whenever I would talk about my cases or medical problems with attorneys or doctors, my mind and body would go through such pain, torture, and other unbelievable problems. The problem of explaining my cases of health issues and problems to professional people and then changing my complete story around and upside down was incredible to unbelievable. It was like they would manufacture their own words and stories to fit their itinerary and leave out the truth of how I explained the complaints and problems to them, which was involved with my information and cases. These problems would happen with all involved with my cases (doctors, attorneys, and eventually, it would include a lot more professional people with their version of my complaints and problems.

Attorney Allen and I would start to have bigger problems between us as time went on. I would also have problems with the doctors not cooperating with the law of this country. Attorney Allen wouldn't like me to look up information from the internet or other sources; one of those sources would be other attorneys. I would start looking for attorneys for malpractice of legal and medical problems. I would start looking because Attorney Allen and the doctors were just rewriting the laws of this country and doing as they please with the laws and with my cases and health problems. They tell me that the information about Robert doesn't matter with my cases or my health problems. If Attorney Allen were telling the truth, I wouldn't be sick or without a job. I got tired of fighting everybody with my legal and medical problems. There is no relief when you have professional people take advantage of me with health problems and legal problems. I need to take back my life and control and take a stand with these professional people. The problems with me taking back control are how much stress and pain I would be under, finding outside help from my cases, and maintaining relations with present professional people. When looking for an attorney who handles malpractice, they have a unique way of discrediting my story and explaining what happened with doctors and attorneys. The problem is when you follow the laws and report all the medical problems and legal problems to the proper authorities. You don't get any good results, only negative results. I would have the task of calling multiple malpractice attorneys and getting no good results.

In Rhode Island, you have a malpractice attorney who doesn't even listen to the complete story from you, and they would refuse the case before its time. So, I would start seeing how malpractice attorneys would protect their kinds of attorneys and doctors. But then, where do you go for justice in this country? Is this country just a big lie with the laws of this country and these people? So, I would look for better avenues with the legal system and government in time. But, I will not give up just because people make things hard for me. Remember, I have lost everything that had a meaning in my life, job, health, and wealth.

CHAPTER 10
Medication and Mental Stress

At the beginning of my problems, the doctors would pass out the medications like candy, especially when the doctors labeled me with mental conditions; the only problem was that I had mental stress problems, and nobody wanted to find an alternative procedure. Mental stress problems are different from other kinds of mental illnesses; my problem was caused by a person bullying, harassing, discriminating, and threatening me as a person. In the early 1900s, electric shock treatments were claimed to help patients with mental illness, but it was only torture for the patients. The families would allow these procedures to happen without knowing the truth of what the doctors were doing or experimenting with their loved ones. The worst part about humans on this planet is that humans will always repeat history in harmful ways by hurting each other humans. We trust professional people who practice medical, legal, and different leadership positions as leaders in our world, countries, states, cities, and towns with terrible results from them in many ways. The best example would be medicine prescribed to help people, but does the medicine work for the best of the patients? Opiates are one of the most dangerous medicines and other drugs pushed by pharmaceutical companies, doctors, and eventually by drug dealers. Even the government and the court judges get in on the profit of allowing pharmaceutical companies to sell harmful drugs to the public with deadly consequences for our people. People were getting addicted to these medicines and drugs with all the companies making a profit and getting rich and powerful companies without any consequences from our United States government. The government received all types of handouts and bribes for money and greed.

When it comes to medications or drugs, very few medications or drugs have helped patients without side effects. Psychological medications are notorious for side effects with conditions that can leave a person in a state of mindlessness in the human body. The other psychological medications would have different side effects; some would make you sleep your day away, suicide effects, muscle issues, paranoia and schizophrenia, and many other problems. Many medicines and drugs with many side effects and deadly conditions and consequences can hurt the human body and mind. Unfortunately, scientists and doctors are giving the OK to use these medications and drugs without knowing the long-term effects on the people. When they find the long-term effects that hurt the people, they will still allow the medicines to be used. The result is a lot of these medications and drugs end up on the streets of America and around the world, with a deadly force of doom for all people of America and worldwide.

The history of medications and drugs speaks very loudly with the knowledge of some injuries related to these medications and drugs. When I started to see the doctors, the medicine was passed out like candy. I would ask the doctors what these medications would do for me. The best answer was it would help you. Once again, I ask the doctors how this will help me. The doctors would reply just take the medications. When I got home, I would look up the medicines on the internet and find a lot of information about medications and how harmful these medications are to people. Some of the medications are progressive medicine, where you start with a low dose to a higher amount within a short time. Then the same progressive medications you take and you cannot just stop with these medications; you can end up dead from stopping these medications. I remembered a commercial on the television from the past saying that they would show a frying pan on the stove, and the person would crack an egg open it, and then say this is your brain on drugs, and it is frying away your brain and your body. This scenario works the same way with all street drugs and all medications. Can medications help people? Yes, but the side effects are the problems, especially when they can leave a person vulnerable in many different ways and dangerous ways; some of the ways are with doctors, attorneys, and just about any way the aggressor wants you to end your life.

When I take the Vicodin pills, I have told the doctors that the medication knocks me out for two days feeling like shit and dopey. Then when I explain taking a muscle relaxer Flexeril pills, this medication does the same as Vicodin and knocks me out for two days feeling like shit and dopey. These medications are for fibromyalgia pain and some other conditions of anxiety problems and IBS cramps. The doctors have tried medications like amitriptyline, gabapentin, duloxetine, and many other related medications for my symptoms of stress-related issues. The medications would confuse my mind and body with all these medications and the shitty feeling that the medication gave me. These medications are non-narcotic, but they carry a punch when I take them somehow. The way medications and drugs affect the mind and body are started from the sensory neurons that send information from the eyes, ears, nose, tongue, and skin to the brain. Motor neurons carry messages away from the brain to the rest of the body. All neurons, however, relay information to each other through a complex electrochemical process, making connections that affect the way we think, learn, move, and behave. Which also leads to joint pain, muscle pain, chest pain, and many other pain problems. Fibromyalgia can affect the complete nervous system starting with sensory neurons to the central nervous system, affecting the whole body (Brain, heart, all the organs within the chest area, and then muscles and joints, including the spine). The central nervous system is compromised so that everyday tasks are an issue and problem.

When I watch television and see the commercials about medications and how these medications can help you and hurt you, the information is given in these commercials about the side effects that medications can cause you. These are heart attacks or heart problems, stroke, seizures, dizziness, making you dopey or sleepy, affecting the organs somehow, and psychologically affecting you. The controversy of the issues and problems, are you safe regarding medications? When you take medications and go into the public world and then operate machines, vehicles, or just about anything that can hurt someone else, you are the one responsible for the laws of this country. Remember, scientists, pharmaceutical companies, and doctors are not responsible for your actions taking these medications, only you.

The controversy with the facts of the medications giving the warning not to do anything work-related and then your job doesn't understand the medications that you have to take. Then your job says that you are fired from your job if you come to work under the influence. When a person does not listen to their boss and goes to work under the influence of any medications or other drugs, then only you are responsible for the laws of operating machinery or vehicles and have accidents or legal problems of breaking our laws. None of the systems like medical, laws and courts, and employment jobs work together when someone is hurt or affected by health problems. Instead, they tell you to take medications and go to work under the influence of medications, and then you break the laws of this country. Our lovely government created a controversy that all the systems don't work together when a person has an illness. Then the person ends up with all types of problems on all levels. There is a new medication for people who take psychological medications. There is a new medicine that helps people with the side effects of the ongoing psychological medicine and treatment they are using at the time. The ongoing problem with all medicines for psychological problems causes body cramps and other issues. The new medicine will stop that problem with another type of side effects added on with these ongoing medications. The way people deal with their issues of being on medications and missing work or risking a chance of going out to work under the influence of medicine is always wrong. Making these mistakes when a person's health is at risk or the public safety is at stake. Also, family and financial issues become a problem when you miss work and then break the law for taking a chance to go to work. The whole picture of different areas of the law, medications, jobs, and needing financial earning is very difficult and controversial with everything involved with these areas that don't work together and protect the person or people in the process of life.

CHAPTER 11
Primary Care

I saw Dr. Lori Iceberg about a year before the incident with the town of Butland. When I first visited Dr. Lori Iceberg (8/18/2014) about my new health conditions, I explained that I had had stomach pains for about two weeks back from today's date. Dr. Lori asked if there were any changes in my life. I explained that everything was fine, not thinking of work problems or the IBS problems. Dr. Lori said I'll send you to Dr. Kenneth Sole, a gastrologist doctor, and see what issues arise. Meanwhile, I'll run some bloodwork and come back in one week for you to see me. I ask for a letter for work. Dr. Lori said, " Do you need a note for the job; I said, yes, that is the new requirement for employment in today's world. I also said that if I stay home for a week, my job needs a reason for what is wrong with my health. So Dr. Lori gives me a letter about my job with very little information to explain my problems with my job. I would turn in the first letter to my job to the ZYX office on the same day I saw the doctor.

I would see the gastrologist doctor within the week of being excused from work. Dr. Kenneth saw me, and he asked what are your problems with you today. I said about two weeks of stomach pains. Dr. Kenneth asked if Dr. Lori did bloodwork, and I said yes. Dr. Kenneth said let's look at your records. Dr. Kenneth said I see you have IBS syndrome, and your bloodwork looks good. Dr. Kenneth asked how I received the IBS problems; I said I was poisoned with the peanut butter poisoning problem in 2008. Dr. Kenneth said that this is your problem; the IBS is acting upon you. I said I don't think so because I normally have diarrhea when IBS acts up. I had no diarrhea for the first two weeks until I started seeing the doctors and worried about my job. Dr. Kenneth asked if I was out of work; I said yes for a week, then saw Dr. Lori. Dr. Kenneth said OK, see her, and I will make an appointment for a month. I said OK. Dr. Kenneth asked if Dr. Lori noticed the IBS problems in your records; I said I don't know. Dr. Kenneth said, " Remind Dr. Lori about your IBS problems with your stomach. I said, OK.

One week passed, and I saw Dr. Lori. She would ask how things with my stomach were. I said that I was getting more pain and starting diarrhea problems. I said that Dr. Kenneth said to remind you about the IBS problems. Dr. Lori ignores the IBS problems and the fact of how Dr. Kenneth told me to tell Dr. Lori. Dr. Lori asks how bad is diarrhea. I said that I have brown water coming out, which is all the time, especially when I drink and eat. Dr. Lori said your bloodwork is normal, and I don't know what I can do for you. I said Well, I am in a lot of pain and diarrhea. I said from one week ago I have got worse. Dr. Lori said let's wait another week and see if the pain and diarrhea stop. I said OK, and I need another letter for work to excuse me again; this would be the second letter. Dr. Lori asks me what kind of work do you do? I said that I work for the town of Butland with the ZYX office. She then asked how long you had been working there. I said almost a year now as an employee, and I have plowed for the town since 2002. Dr. Lori said here is the letter, and I will see you in one week. As I was leaving her office, I started to think about her questions about my job; she knew when I started my job with the town. I couldn't understand why at this time, but eventually I did find out why she questioned my job. I turned in the second letter to my job from Dr. Lori excusing me from work.

I would see secretary Wendy and pass in the doctor's letter. As I talked to Wendy about work and the letter, I started to have health problems. I said to Wendy I'm not feeling good. I needed to call the doctor; Wendy asked if I was OK; I said no, I needed to go, and I'll keep in touch and update you. So I would leave the ZYX office and go home to call Dr. Lori. When Dr. Lori called me back, I explained that I was turning in the letter and I had started having health problems. Dr. Lori asked what are the symptoms I said chest pains, headaches, my heart pounding, confusion and loss feeling, body pains throughout my body, and other problems. Dr. Lori said that you have an anxiety attack with panic attacks. Dr. Lori said you need to lay down and rest or you need to go to the hospital, and I will see you next week for your appointment. When I hung up with the doctor, I thought this woman understood my problems and knew I had anxiety problems. My world was falling apart because of a boss and now my health.

I would see Dr. Lori within the second week of being out of work. Dr. Lori would ask how things were with me; I said getting worse with headaches, pounding heart, body aches, confusion, dizziness, IBS cramps and diarrhea, and many other problems. Dr. Lori said I want you to see a psychiatrist Dr. Jen Chow and therapist counselor Fay Pain. I asked why I would see them. Dr. Lori said they would help you with mental stress and anxiety problems. So, I said that means I have mental stress problems Dr. Lori said yes, you have anxiety plus more issues that need to be addressed with a psychiatrist, doctors, and therapist counselors. I will give you another week out of work till you see Dr. Jen Chow and therapist Fay Pain. I said I would need another excused letter for my job and explained what was wrong with me in this third letter to protect my job. I left the room and went to the front desk to set another appointment with Dr. Lori and pick up my excused letter for work. When I received the letter, there was no explanation of my health issues for my job. I started having anxiety attacks from this letter that had no information about my health or to explain things for my job. The doctor has created a bigger problem with my job, not just once but three times, now with these letters not explaining the seriousness of my problems. I had to drive home with this anxiety attack and then have my daughter Jenny take the letter in for me to my job.

When my daughter Jenny got to my job at the ZYX office, she went in to see secretary Wendy Potts. Jenny told Wendy I have an excused letter for my father, Vince, excusing him from work at the doctor's office. Wendy said to Jenny that I needed to call Robert. When Wendy called Robert, Robert went crazy over the phone with Wendy, and Jenny could hear everything Robert was saying about me and work. My daughter couldn't believe her ears; Robert was like a madman, like a DR. Jekyll and Mr. Hyde. Robert was screaming that he would not accept this letter or any other letters from the doctors; the doctors weren't even explaining his health problems in the letters. Robert said that Mr. Vincent D'Angelo had been dismissed from his job, and if he wanted his check, he needed to return his uniforms in person, and his paycheck would be given to him only. Jenny would say ok, I will tell my father what you said about him and his job, Jenny would leave the office intimidated by Robert and how he was screaming. Jenny would head home to our house; at the same time, Robert would call me with a harassing and intimidating voice, saying that I was excused from my job. I said what are you talking about, Robert? My daughter is turning in the doctor's letter, and you can't dismiss me from my job being sick or with an illness. I asked what the reasons for releasing me from my job were. Robert would not answer my question about why I was released from my job. I said OK, Robert, I will see you in court. I hope you like jail because that's where you are going when I'm done with you, and I hung up with Robert.

When my daughter Jenny got home, she began to cry. I said what's wrong? Jenny said that this man Robert was yelling over the phone and I could hear everything he said about you to secretary Wendy. Jenny said that Robert was an evil man to get so crazy over an excuse letter from a doctor. I said to my daughter that's why I have mental stress problems from my job because of one man named Robert. I said that Robert does this to everyone; he bullies the workers and the town residents. He harasses people, discriminates in many different ways against people, lies unbelievable, and sets people (workers) against each other; Jenny, you are right; Robert is an evil man with powers. Jenny said you should take him to court and fight for your rights. I said that Robert would call me after you left the office. We fought over the phone it started as you can't bring in your letters, then he went on to say that I was dismissed from work permanently. Then I asked why, and what was the reason for this and Robert ignored the question. Then I told him off by saying I will see you in court and hang upon him. Jenny said yes, he must have called you after I left the office. Jenny asked if I would contact an attorney; I said yes, I lost my job without valid reasons or excuses.

After the incident with Jenny and Robert and with an anxiety attack from leaving the doctor's office, which is also a reason why I didn't take the letter to the ZYX office, I decided to call Dr. Lori Iceburg for an appointment so that I could explain what happened with my daughter. On the phone call from my boss Robert, I left her office with an anxiety attack. When I called the doctor's office, they gave me an appointment the next day. At the appointment, Dr. Lori asked why I was here; when I saw you yesterday, I said that I had one anxiety attack because your letter didn't explain my health problems, and then I had a second attack with my boss over the phone. Dr. Lori said what do you want me to do? I said that you can connect the dots with my job being a stressful place of work and that my boss is the cause of all of this, and I have a witness to what he did to my daughter. Dr. Lori said this has nothing to do with me as a doctor. I said that you are mandated to make notes about the abuse from people and my boss with all these medical and legal issues if needed. I said you are ignoring the abuse and issues and problems; why? I didn't see your boss treat you this way or your daughter. I said you didn't know about the incident with my boss, but I'm reporting the problem to you and my medical conditions, why I'm sick with mental stress issues, and how it came to me. I said to Dr. Lori are you going to help me with my medical and legal problems? Dr. Lori replied I did with referring you to a psychiatrist and a therapist. I said what about your cooperating with my attorney Allen? Dr. Lori said that is the legal part for an attorney, not for me as a doctor. I said the attorney needs the proper medical information from you as the doctor. Dr. Lori said it's not my problem! This battle would go on for seven years with this doctor with no cooperation from me or my attorney.

When I got home, I called for attorney Allen and started to explain about the doctor and how she explained things to me during my visit with her. I explained that the doctor wasn't going to cooperate with me or you as an attorney and that my medical issues and legal cooperation weren't Dr. Lori's problems. I ask Attorney Allen what we can do about this doctor with lawful means. Attorney Allen said that you are screwed without the doctor being in your corner and having no cases. I said Allen, you, as an attorney, have no laws which can hold her responsible for her actions. Attorney Allen said no, she has free will to do as she pleases with no consequences to her profession. I ended up getting mad with attorney Allen and said you are wrong. I know things about the laws of this country; you aren't fighting for my rights; you are taking advantage of this mental stress that I have. Attorney Allen tried to reassure me about the doctor. I said to Attorney Allen, between the town who was lying and then-Attorney Bob and now Dr. Lori, and now you want me to think with all of these problems except that I'm losing the battle before I get up at bat or with court time. Are you nuts, Allen? I would feel like all involved are taking advantage of a person with handicap problems mental stress health conditions. You disregard my complaints and the true story about the whole situation and everyone involved intentionally dropping the ball and information on my cases. The cases are falling apart with people helping themselves being against me. There are so many ways of discrimination breaking the laws, and hurting the people and me. The sad part is when people say, "Why did he crack or go on a rampage," Well, these are just some reasons. There is a lot more to come in the future in these cases.

CHAPTER 12
Therapy

Dr. Lori Iceberg referred me to psychiatrist Dr. Jen Chow and therapist counselor Fay Pain for mental stress, psychosis, depression, sleep disorder, and many other issues that would come over time with me. I needed all this information for my job, and Dr. Lori wasn't passing this information on to my job or my attorney Allen; we were looking for this information. I now see how; I believe that Dr. Lori started all of these problems with her office with the other doctors and the hospital she works within. When the day came for my appointment with Dr. Jen, she would ask why I was here at her office. I explained that my primary, Dr. Lori referred me because of mental stress from my job and anxiety. Dr. Jen said you are also here for psychosis, depression, sleep disorder, and other issues. I said I did not know all this information; my primary Dr., Lori, didn't explain my health issues. Dr. Jen asked what has happened to you? You are here with me today. I started to explain that I had a job with the town of Butland, and my boss was bullying, harassing, discriminating, and threatening my job and other things with no cause or reason. Which would lead to my stomach hurting for two weeks, and then I called the doctor's office for an appointment with her. I said that I'm fifty years old and have never been released from any job or anything related to me in such a wrong way. Meanwhile, I also have a family that depends on me to provide for them. I planned to retire from this job and finish my life in good condition for my family and me. All of this went down the toilet when my boss started all these problems. I have about 12 years of total time working for this department of the town, and all of this is lost with no backup for work, plus my health problems.

Dr. Jen said I could see how you would feel being betrayed by one man named Robert Smith. Dr. Jen asked how the other workers were with you; I said we all got along and remembered 12 years working with these men. Here is another reason I can't understand why Robert would do what he did to me. Dr. Jen asked how my family's relationship is. I just said that they depend on me but otherwise, it's suitable for a family. Dr. Jen said all of your problems are from your job and nowhere else. I told her, yes, my job only, but really it is with my boss Robert; he gives me the hardest times, not the workers. Dr. Jen said I must have a hard time believing that only my job did this to me. I asked, what did she mean. She said, we will talk about this the next time you come here in a week, but for now, I will give you some medications to help you. Dr. Jen asked if I was seeing a therapist; I said yes, in Fay Pain's office. Dr. Jen said yes, I know her. Will you be seeing her soon? I said yes, tomorrow; Dr. Jen said I would talk to her about you. I asked Dr. Jen what the medicine would do to me. Dr. Jen said that it would calm you down, so you are at ease with yourself, and let you sleep at night. I said that Dr. Lori gave me some medicine for the same reasons, and the medicine didn't help me. Dr. Jen said OK, just take this medicine, and next week, we will see if you are ok with the medicine. Dr. Jen said I would see you in a week same time.

The next day I would see therapist Fay Pain, and we would go through the introductions and the questions of why, how, when, whom, and the regular information they need to have to evaluate the patient. I explained the same story and complaints to Fay as to Dr. Jen and many other doctors and attorneys. Then Fay said that I spoke to Dr. Jen, and we came out with a plan for us to come together next week and talk together for a session. I asked if this was a standard procedure. Fay said that Dr. Jen and I need to understand the issues and to know the same story from you. I said that I only told the truth from the beginning and that many people involved with this whole case are screwing things up. Fay said that it's not the problem, we had a conversation and how excited you are, and we are worried about you and your health. I said, " Are you sure about what you just explained, or are you scared that I will hurt you or Dr. Jen? I said that I don't believe in hurting people unless I'm defending my life at a physical level from a fight. I have been hurt by everybody involved in my cases. And that this hasn't stopped with all the people I'm dealing with, and now with both of you. If I were to hurt anyone, it would be the person that started these problems. But it doesn't stop my stress with that person or all the people involved and adds more problems by denying my medical and legal problems and then making me feel like I'm the crazy one here. The most important reason I don't hurt anyone is that I have two cases involving lawsuits; I'm not going to jail for the wrong reasons. Fay said OK, for now, we will talk about this next week with Dr. Jen and us together.

The following week came, and I would see Dr. Jen and Fay together for a meeting. During this meeting, I would discover things nobody would believe, including me, even though I was there. The mental abuse in this country is very overwhelming, and it's on every level of society, for example, families, jobs, our government, etc. The meeting started, and Dr. Jen started to ask me if my father abused me; I said what does this have to do with the facts of my job and my boss? I got no answers from Dr. Jen.

Dr. Jen then asked whether I was sexually abused by my father or anyone else. Once again, I wondered what this had to do with my job or my boss. I got no answers again.

Then Dr. Jen and Fay started to double-team with questions about my family, and it seemed like they were trying to break me by giving in to their drilling tactics. This is where I said what the hell are you trying to do to me? I said my family is not the issues or problems with my health; it is only my job and boss. I also said that if you call this helping me, you are both wrong; you are only causing more stress to me at this point. I asked if they understood why I was there looking for help. I got no answers again. Dr. Jen asked if I was taking medicine I prescribed to you; I said no; what are you trying to do, keeping me under the influence of drugs so that I have no common sense in my mind or my complaints about the town and my boss. All of you doctors pass out the medicine like it was candy; you're worse than the drug dealers from the streets. Dr. Jen said if you don't take medicine, then I can't see you; I said fine!!!, I'm all done with you; you accused my family of lies when the problem was my job and boss only.

The problem is I have no trust in any professional people; how else can a man think when a doctor tries to say my family was involved with abuse when the complaints were against the town of Butland and Robert Smith? So on a mental level, in my mind, I want to hurt the people who have put me in this position and condition of stress and pain with many other problems. The rage inside me was so hard to control, but leaving the office would help me get over the feeling of calming down and putting things in perspective for myself and my future with these people and my cases.

About a week later, I received a phone call from therapist Fay asking me if I would make an appointment to see her. I asked why I should. Fay said so you could talk about your problems and issues. I said, " Are you going to attack me with lies and other difficulties; Fay said, no, I want to help you; that meeting was Dr. Jen's idea because she believed you were hiding problems with your family. I told Fay that I told Dr. Jen that it was because of work reasons only; I'm here otherwise because my primary Dr. Lori referred me to you people. I don't understand how things got so screwed up with the information I gave all the people involved with my cases. Fay asked again if I would like to come to the office. She said she'd try to help you with your problems. I would agree with going to the office for a visit to talk about my problems. My stress was so built up inside me that I started to have pain running throughout my body. The headaches, joint pains, stabbing pains, neck and back pains were going up and down my spine, and my muscles were cramping up so bad I didn't know what to do except call the Fire Deptartment of Butland.

I was rushed to the hospital in Brock and was seen by the doctors there. The doctors would do their testing to determine what was wrong with me. The doctors said that I have all stress-related issues, but I have one new problem, fibromyalgia; with these stress issues, you will have pain that will worsen over time. The doctors said I needed to take a muscle relaxer and vidicon for pain. I explained to the doctors at the hospital that I was susceptible to medication. The doctors explain that because of fibromyalgia is why you are so sensitive to medications. The doctors said that a website would explain your stress issues and look for fibromyalgia problems on the C.D.C. website. You need to rest and take medicine till you handle your stress problems. The doctors asked if I was seeing anyone for therapy; I said, yes, ok, we will notify them, Dr. Lori and Fay Pain, and let them know you were here for stress-related issues. You'll have to wait to see them because of the medicines; maybe a month's wait for a visit.

I would be released from the hospital, and I would have to do a follow-up with primary Dr. Lori. I would also have to call therapist Fay to reschedule an appointment later. I went to my appointment with Dr. Lori. I asked her about this issue of fibromyalgia, and Dr. Lori said that she doesn't believe in this medical issue, and other doctors also don't believe this fibromyalgia. I said that this fibromyalgia issue is seen in the medical books as a stress-related problem and a mental stress disorder. Dr. Lori would avoid the questions and say is there anything else I can do for you. I said yes; I went to the hospital, and they told me to have a follow-up with you. I ask you about this fibromyalgia, and you just blow me off like I don't exist, then you tell me that you don't believe in this medical issue acknowledged in the medical books and C.D.C. website. I asked what kind of a doctor are you that doesn't help out your patients, especially when there are two legal cases involving an attorney. You don't give the proper medical records and information to the attorney or me. If I change doctors, the town attorneys would say that I'm shopping for new doctors that will go in their favor in court. Then the judges just frown upon these issues when they hear these things against me and rule against me with a loss in the courts. I also said that this is also part of the stress you are causing with all my problems.

Dr. Lori said you can always change doctors if you're not happy with me. I don't believe you are so unreal; I said I'm done with today's visit myself. Dr. Lori said I'll see you in three months and your referral to Dr. Peter Orlando. I asked what choice do I have. Once again, the fury and rage that ran through my body were incredible; with all the stress and pain from Dr. Lori, I had to find a way of calming myself down without getting into trouble. I thought of music to calm me down as I went home; music has always helped me throughout my life in so many different ways. The feeling of music is so incredible for healing, happiness, expressing your love, when you are sad, many other ways, and of course when you have parties and good times. The sound of music would help me control the stress and the aggravation of these professional people who were intentionally throwing my health around with no care in the world and what could happen to me.

CHAPTER 13
More Therapy

I would call attorney Allen to report all new information about my health and Dr. Lori. I explained to Attorney Allen that this doctor was not good. Attorney Allen said you still need her for the records and medical information. I said she was not working with us, but she was working against us; there must be a way to report Dr. Lori to authorities about these criminal actions. I told Allen that Dr. Lori is the principal and primary doctor controlling my medical needs. Then I told Allen that the psychiatrist, Dr. Jen, tried to suggest, accuse, and insist that all of what I'm going through is related to my father and family. I said we have problems with all of these doctors that I need you to correct with the proper authorities about all of these doctors. Attorney Allen said there is nothing I can do for you; all I can do is go forward with the information we have with the courts.

I said that we don't even have a chance of winning these cases because of not having enough medical information and records and depending on doctors who aren't following the laws and cooperating with us. I thought for a moment and then asked Attorney Allen, what are the chances of the town having any influence with these doctors and you as my attorney? Attorney Allen said that it was against the law for the town to do those dirty deeds. I told Allen that I was talking about the doctors alone with breaking the laws. I said Allen, I know that people can be bribed, especially regarding money issues and paying less without proper judgment against them. Attorney Allen would avoid these questions and answers that I asked him. Attorney Allen would say that he has another thing to work on; if more problems arise, give me a call. The sad part of people's history, especially doctors, law enforcement, our country's presidents, etc., have been bribed throughout history. It all comes down to money and power, with greed destroying all the people worldwide and beyond.

    I would ask for my family to come together so that we could talk about the issues of my case and get advice and guidance. We would start by discussing with Attorney Allen first all the questions and explanations that Attorney Allen said to me during the office visits. My mother said I couldn't believe what you are going through with this attorney Allen. My brother Joseph said it is illegal for what you are going through. You should report them to legal authorities. If I do that, I said I'm rocking the boat, and the attorney could walk away. My sisters Sarah and Anthony said you are between a rock and a hard place. Anthony would say change attorneys; I said that money would be the issue I don't have. I said that the doctors have a lot to do with this. Without the proper medical evidence and records going to the attorney, the cases will be lost. Joseph said how long you have been bounced around with these people at this point? I said about three years ago. Then try to just get through these cases and get the best you can change all of the people involved, start with new professional people, or report the issues, problems, and crimes to law enforcement. My mother would then say you can't beat city hall; I would get upset with my mother and say that I don't accept those conditions; the law is made to protect the innocent, righteous, and justice. I have a hard time believing that people are above the laws and justice. I will try to follow the laws to the total capacity of the laws of this country. I will get justice one way or another by following the laws.

I said simultaneously; I have been dealing with all that has happened for three years. My symptoms are going out of control with anxiety, IBS, depression, psychosis, and new symptoms of fibromyalgia and all the side effects of the main symptoms. Plus a lot of other new problems will come in time. I have trouble trusting the doctors, attorneys, and everyone with no accurate information about my medical conditions and not passing medical information on to my attorney Allen. Attorney Allen does not fight hard enough for his client or put up grievances against the town and their attorneys and doctors. I gave the true story, and complaints from me, and professional people are changing the story from the original status and truth to lies and being deceived in so many ways. Starting with Robert and the town together with their version of lies, that has altered these cases from the beginning. To all attorneys with their version of lies and falsifying legal records. With the original complaints and stories and the doctors lying about medical records, my mental health was affected on so many levels. It was like my mind would explode with all the pressure from all of these lies from professional people. The worst part of these problems is that nobody wanted to hold Robert and the town of Butland responsible for the lies because of money responsibility and fault for the issues and problems they gave me. Another reason is that nobody wants to report any criminal actions against the professional people involved. It can come back at them as they break the laws themselves, so everybody will be quiet about the main problems of criminal actions and get away from prosecution of our laws.

I would have an appointment with Dr. Peter Orlando, the rheumatologist. Dr. Peter is for arthritis and my condition of fibromyalgia. Dr. Peter would ask what was wrong with me; I said I had arthritis and fibromyalgia; fibromyalgia is the new problem with my health conditions. Dr. Peter said you also have anxiety, depression, body pains, joint pains, psychosis, headaches, and other problems. I said yes, doctor, everything I have is stress-related and that this started with my boss Robert being a bully and abuser. Dr. Peter avoided the explanation I gave him about my boss and my job. I explained to Dr. Peter that fibromyalgia pain is killing my hands, feet, and spine with my headaches. Secondary pain is with my muscles, chest pains, scalp hurt to touch or brush my hair, jaw pains, and other issues. Dr. Peter said that some of these conditions overlap, and some don't overlap your conditions. Dr. Peter said that you have arthritis in the hands, feet, and joints, and fibromyalgia affects your hands, feet, and joints.

The headaches and spine are other stories; we will have to watch your conditions and your body to find out which one has presented over the other. Dr. Peter said I don't believe in this fibromyalgia; I said that this fibromyalgia is in the medical books and that you don't believe in this health problem. What about the fact that all of my conditions are stress-related? They work off each other to intensify the issues and pains. Dr. Peter said yes, stress-related conditions could intensify from other stress-related disorders. If that is the case, then this is how fibromyalgia is working overtime with the pain and stress. Plus, add that I have been fighting everybody with these cases doctors, attorneys, Robert, and the town of Butland with their lies and changing the complaint around and against me. Dr. Peter said that had nothing to do with me; I said what? Yes, it does because I'm sick from stress, and the fact of stress related to work conditions and problems and from professional people involved with my cases gives an impossible time to me and my health. Dr. Peter just avoids the statement I just said to him. I'll give you some medicine for your pain and to relax you. I said that I have a lot of prescriptions that do the same thing and that I have a lot of sensitivity to all the medicine; I was told that it's because of fibromyalgia and how it affects my nervous system. Once again, the conversation was just avoided. Dr. Peter said I would see you in three months, and I left the office so upset with another doctor again.

My third appointment came up with therapist Fay. We both greeted each other, and she asked how I was doing. I said not so good; Fay asked why. I said I was fighting with everybody involved with me and my cases. Fay would say do you think it's because you are the problem and not cooperating with people. I said no, it's because people are trying to push buttons and then push me off the cliff's edge like I'm the crazy one and not them for lying about the complaints. People are intentionally pushing my buttons for me to retaliate and break the laws and get me committed for mental issues. I saw how things work for people in my shoes with no chance and getting arrested for defending themselves. Nobody listens to my complaints of abuse and a stressful condition from Robert and the town, and then everybody after that (doctors, attorneys). People protect Robert and the town and leave me in the dark like I don't exist. These people damage a person, and it's okay for them to do this damage and get away with it. Fay would say that people are trying to help you, and you aren't seeing that way. I said, well, with what happened with Dr. Jen and accusing my father and family of things and lies, then yes, I have the problems.

Fay said that you misunderstood the whole situation of the questions. Fay said I need to ask you some questions, and then I need you to fill out a computer questionnaire. Fay asked if I wanted to hurt myself; I said no, then asked if I would hurt anyone else; I said no; why would you ask stupid questions? I told you I'm not a violent man like that; I only believed in defending myself when needed on a physical level. I said this is the perfect example of what I just explained to you about people pushing the button intentionally for a reaction from me to violate the laws. Fay would say that we are not trying to hurt you; we are only trying to help you. I said we would see the truth in time. Fay would give me a computer to take a questionnaire. This questionnaire had like 40 questions, and it asked if I would hurt someone or myself in separate questions. In time Fay would use this computer questionnaire against me and betray me for a second time.

I would look for guidance from my family again and throughout the time of my problems with these cases. I would always have a family member with me when I visited the doctors and attorneys, but sometimes I would have to be on my own. One of those times, I would be alone with therapist Fay; it was difficult for the family to get away from their obligations every week. Nobody in my family would ever think that a therapist would turn against me in any way, shape, or form. My family and I started to see that I would have any problems with these cases and the professional people involved. I would always tell my family how the therapist would explain things to me and how she would flip things around on me. The dire situation is that I needed to see a therapist for the cases because attorney Allen said you don't have a case without a therapist. The hardest thing is that nobody wants to cooperate with any part of my problems or that professional people intentionally fail the cases and me. My family tried to help me the best they could. Still, lies, manipulation, false information, and many other ways of changing the actual outcome of cases are impossible when you are going up against professional people. When I look up the definition of discrimination, it says:

An act or instance of discriminating or of making a distinction.

Treatment or consideration of, or making a distinction in favor of or against, a person or thing based on the group, class, or category to which that person or thing belongs rather than on individual merit:

The power of making fine distinctions; discriminating judgment:

Archaic. Something that serves to differentiate.

Laws don't explain the right ways to the people; the laws only have categories, and if it doesn't fit into categories, it's not discrimination. These would work the same way with many laws that don't fit the categories and many other areas like the medical profession and many other systems we have. Plus, it's incredible how people fit the laws to their needs and not for the common good of the public of the world. The minute that the law doesn't follow the proper laws when chaos and anarchy start to creep in and take over the people and land. The truth for any human being is that we all want revenge when people do wrong to people. Then the people who started the problem don't expect this person to push back against the person who harmed the person or other people. We must have proper laws for our land and the people within our world. But when you have people who can change the laws to fit themselves or circumstances. People fixing the laws is another part of discrimination that follows and other laws broken by the individual and anyone. Individual merit is precisely how the laws forget that individual people discriminate against each other. Significantly when the laws and officials discriminate directly against ordinary citizens, individuals, and groups, I would always look for better answers to my legal and proper problems for the people of our country. I've never liked people who lied, cheat, or steal, and many other crimes are worse than you imagine in your mind unless you are a criminal.

The seven cardinal sins of this world are:

Pride

Greed

Lust

Envy

Gluttony

Wrath

Sloth

Each of these can be overcome with the seven corresponding virtues:

Humility

Charity

Chastity

Gratitude

Temperance

Patience

Diligence

I acknowledge the seven cardinal sins of the world but is anyone involved with my cases? The best thing about a person is when they have the correct answers patience, and diligence with their lives or cases.

In time, people will show their true colors, who will be right or wrong, who is good or bad, a criminal or good citizen who told the truth, and nobody wants to hear the truth. I just won't accept that the official authorities or people are criminals. Still, the reality of history is that men, women, and children will always commit criminal actions over their lifetime. I know I'm no angel in this world, but I try my hardest to follow our existing laws and the proper ways of this land and people. However, when I have to defend my life or my family's lives, am I being the lawbreaker, am I doing the right thing, or am I being ignorant of the laws and the people? I will question my actions even if I am following the laws of this country and the people. The human conscience is a powerful inner feeling about yourself that helps you make the right decision in your life and for other lives. I would learn how in time, I know that I have to defend myself against Robert, the town, doctors, attorneys, and anyone in future my cases.

Dark Justice White Collar Crimes

CHAPTER 14

Writing Letters and Reporting Crimes

I would take the advice from my family to report the issues, problems, and crimes to the proper authorities, or so I thought. I wasn't the best writer for this task, but I was the only one who could tell the true story and complaints. I have different health problems that will interfere with my writing these letters because of multiple health issues starting with anxiety. Writing these letters is like reliving the abuses, harassment, verbal abuse, plus discrimination from starting with Robert to the present time. Then the lies and problems from the doctors and attorneys made my situation worse for me with the health problems and dealing with life every day. Then, after all the lies that turn me into a perpetrator in some crazy or criminal way against Robert, the town, doctors, and attorneys. The sad part is the facts and evidence would prove that Robert and the town were lying instead of me; let's not forget doctors and attorneys and the abuse from them of not upholding the laws of a patient and client. It's tough to concentrate on anything around you when you have anxiety attacks and other stress-related health issues; your mind bounces inside your skull, and your heart bangs like drums. Then you lose your breath, gasping for air; now the pain starts kicking in all over your body. Then your stomach makes you run to the bathroom because of diarrhea and cramps. Fibromyalgia then starts its message to the body; the feeling is like someone crumbling your body like a piece of paper, and you have no way of stopping the pain that you could never imagine, in any way, shape, or form; it was killing pain beyond hell.

Now let's explain the problems of sleeping, sitting, standing, walking, and everything that can happen with your body; when a person can't lose the pain, you start thinking of suicide to relieve distress. Your head is ready to explode from the headaches; then, the stabbing pains will begin with someone pulling on your joints that feel like they are ripping the joints from your body. I would do all of this work in writing these letters with no medicine except for Advil pills or Ibuprofen pills to dull my pains. When I did use the pain medicine Vicodin and a muscle relaxer Flexeril it would make me feel like I wasn't in this world, like I was in a fog of never-ending. It was related to fibromyalgia and how the nervous system works with drugs, prescriptions, or street drugs, including alcohol. The way Dr. Peter explains it is like your nervous system is like a house with wiring, and the lights are turned on forever with no off time. Eventually, your nervous system will burn out somehow, and I'm not sure how this will happen, he would explain to me. Over time, you will become a prescription user and be hospitalized because of how badly your body will suffer from fibromyalgia.

You now know how much my health has been compromised in just about 3.5 years, and Dr. Peter said it would only worsen from the beginning. My problems are only halfway through 7 years, and what will happen after seven years or when I'm older? These are some of the letters that I wrote to the authorities. The first set of letters was given to the

Governor of Rhode Island, the Attorney General of Rhode Island, the Federal Justice Department Washington D.C., Sealand office of the Federal Justice Department, Norfolk DA of Norfolk County, Suffolk DA of Suffolk County, with two Rhode Island Senators and the four main news stations in Rhode Island asking them for help and trying to report the criminal acts of these people which is Robert, town, attorneys, and doctors. Over time, judges will get involved with these cases, with their judgments and devastating answers. I blame the judges entirely and directly, but they can also be held responsible for trusting and not looking into any problems with bad attorneys, wrong doctors, insufficient information, and medical and legal records that were not legal and were given to these judges. When these bad attorneys, wrong doctors, and inadequate information, medical and legal records would lie, deceive, and mislead these judges for bad results and bad judgments against innocents of my cases and me. I would try to explain to these judges the trustworthy information, and these judges told me to let the attorneys handle the cases and not you. I was disregarded by these judges, who also made things more difficult for me to stand up for my rights as a person with all attorneys against me and involved with these cases. Now I am being prosecuted or poorly treated by the attorneys as the bad guy when the attorneys have their guilt and faults for all these problems of these cases. I will guess an unwritten law says that you don't report the criminals or crimes to authorities in this country or deal with the destructive results of your reported problems. I have been painted as a wrong person trying to stand up for my rights and the people of this country, with doctors, attorneys, judges, and all involved. I got no results with the first set of letters; this would only crush me and make things harder to handle with my health problems.

  My anxiety and health problems only worsened when I tried to follow the laws and got no results with my letter reports. The pain of fibromyalgia would come on more potent as well over time. I would take time to try to heal myself when the doctors didn't want to cure me; the doctors only wanted to give me medicines that didn't help and would have side effects that would make me useless as a person. Between the doctors and attorneys, I would think about how to fix or heal myself in the best of ways. One of the ways of trying would take me to a mental level of healing and then a physical level of healing. Another way is to look up as much information about my health conditions and the laws of this country. I would go through all my memories and the problems from my cases and the professional people involved with two cases and problems. I was going to make sure that the public would know the truth about our government, attorneys, doctors, and our law system with all the criminals that are professional people hurting the people and isolating people like me. I would do things to help keep my mind busy and not concentrate on the cases and problems of the cases. I would spend time listening to the music that I grew up with; they say that music has healing powers that doctors don't know about or care about for their patients. I like to listen to and sing along with my music which helps me emotionally. Then on a physical level, it motivates me to clean the house, cut the lawn, and stay busy following a day-to-day schedule. I needed to improve myself and fight harder, mentally and physically, especially when my attorney wasn't doing the job he was paid to do the right way; in other words, he was only stealing my money and doing nothing for me or my cases. I would also go through my memories of my dad and his teachings when I was a child and before my dad passed away. My dad always knew that I wouldn't stop until I proved people wrong with whatever they were doing wrong. Sometimes my dad would say let it go. It's not worth the reason for arguing, even if you are right, but my dad always knew that I wouldn't do that and not let go. My dad knew I would fight till the end and prove that I was right with anyone for the right reason and beyond that reason. My family and I had a strong bond, and nobody could break that bond. The strange thing about Italians is they can hurt each other but don't ever jump between them. You will have two Italian people fighting you.

The music of my days growing up was the best music in the world. I remember from the 40s up to the present. But the music from the '60s to '80s would share the feelings of singers and bands that would express their feelings, and you could also express your feelings on different occasions. Music would help me with my anxiety and get my mind to try to concentrate on what was important to me and my cases. Listening to music also helps me write better letters later in time. I would get my mind together and more stabilized, which gave me hope of fighting these people on their level of bull shit (lying, deceiving, misleading) to come prepared for the actual story. I was being forced to accept their illegal answers and judgments, and I was going to challenge them on their level and become my attorney with their proper laws of answers. It would give me the greatest hope of all; I also decided to write a second letter to all of these official authorities that I have written before with a better letter and words to explain the issues, problems, and criminal acts. I would believe that I would win the decisions of the proper laws and the honest people within law enforcement.

I would write the second letter with all of the issues of health problems and criminal matters. The time of days that it takes me to write letters, someone else could have done in one day. I would have to use a dictionary and computer spelling & grammar to succeed in writing these letters. I would put so much effort and time into these letters that I was so relieved and proud that I sent them out as soon as possible when I finished them. I was prouder of these letters than the first set of letters that I wrote. Once more, I would wait for a phone call, e-mail, or letter with no response or answer after days, weeks, and then months. Once more, I would feel like authorities were protecting these doctors, attorneys, judges, and even their own "authorities" that I was reporting. Amazingly, the police and politicians want the public to follow the laws, but when it comes to themselves, following the laws just disappears for them, and they get away with breaking the laws of this country. I noticed that the politicians didn't like the rush on their capital building in Washington D.C. so why do you tread on the public and their hardships? The police have a neighborhood watch for crimes; maybe the public should have politicians watch for politicians' crimes. Perhaps the public should have a website for the crimes of the rich & powerful, which includes the high society along with the lawmakers and enforcement; what is good for one citizen is good for all citizens, no matter your status in this world. If not, the way I said it, then you, as the leaders of society, are the world's most prominent criminals.

CHAPTER 15
Doctor Visits

I had an appointment with Dr. Lori, and she asked me how I've been doing; I explained that my headaches are too much pain, body pains and muscle pain with cramps, back is hurting along with my spine, hands, and feet pain, having a hard time sleeping with this pain running throughout my body. I'm in pain 24/7, but when the night comes, the pain increases unbelievably; then, when the weather gets cold and when the weather changes with rain, snow, and cold, I go out of my mind with pain. I told myself that I was losing my mind with all of this pain I had lived with for about 3.5 years and worried about future pains. Dr. Lori asked if I was seeing therapist Fay. I said yes. Dr. Lori asks if I've been taking medicine to help you; I explain yes to some and no to others. The psychological pills, no; I take Advil and ibuprofen for pain, and when the pain is too much to handle, maybe Vidicon and muscle relaxer Flexeril. When I take Vidicon and Flexeril, I'm knocked out for two days; I told you I'm sensitive to the medicine because of how the medication affects the receptors in the brain with fibromyalgia. Dr. Lori said if you don't take psychological medicine, there is nothing more I can do for you. I told Dr. Lori that I'm having problems with Vidicon and Flexeril after being knocked out for two days, and you want me to use the other medicine, not knowing what will happen with these medicines. I said you are a crazy doctor. My problems are turning into physical problems with the body pain and not mental problems at this point. I said Dr. Lori; you know that I am in so much pain; why haven't you sent me to a pain management doctor? Dr. Lori would only avoid me and my question. Then I said what are you trying to do to me? When you avoid other doctors who could help me out medically, legally, and personally. Then I said that my father and brother have mesothelioma. Can you give me a test to find out if I have mesothelioma? Dr. Lori said no, you are fine. Then I said you prescribe Zantac for my stomach pains and gas. This medicine has been recalled; this medicine has been linked to cancer problems. Are you going to test me for this problem?

Dr. Lori said no, your x-rays show no cancer with either matter. I asked when these x-rays were taken; about a year back or longer? Dr. Lori said about that time. I said OK, but my brother just found out recently, and I have worked construction all of my life, so don't you think I should be tested for mesothelioma? Dr. Lori said no, you're fine. I turned around and said, Dr. Lori, you really don't care about your patients, or is it just me? Dr. Lori would say, "I will see you in six months." Leaving Dr. Lori's office, I started to think that she would be useless as a doctor, and I would report her to the medical board. I would start avoiding the office visits with Dr. Lori, only going there when I needed to. I couldn't leave this doctor because of the attorneys and courts, doctor shopping, and how they used it against people or victims of criminal matters or court cases.

The same week I had an appointment with therapist Fay. When I got to the office, I had to fill out a computer questionnaire first, and then I would see Fay. When I went into her office, she looked up the computer questionnaire. Fay explains that the computer says that you aren't getting better. I asked what you meant; Fay said you were bottoming out on the computer questionnaire. What does that mean to me? Fay said, "You are on a suicide trip or you will hurt the people who did you wrong." I said you are nuts! I told you there is too much money involved with the lawsuits, and I'm not going to jail for a dumb reason for hurting someone or myself.

What does a computer have over you that you can see visually? Do you think I would hurt or kill someone? Fay would avoid the question. When the computer asks me questions, if I would hurt myself or someone, I have always said no to those questions with the computer. So, where are you getting your information from Fay? I have seen you for about 1.5 years, and the computer has always said that you will hurt yourself and others. I said I'm sorry you let the computer decide my faith with my health conditions. I said that if I were to be a killer, I wouldn't seek help to start, I wouldn't care about a lawsuit, and I wouldn't be fighting with everybody to prove that the town was wrong legally. So that means that your computer is 100% wrong, or you were told to take these actions? I said, OK, I'm leaving because your mind is made up, and that is fine. I would walk out of the office and go home. I would tell my mother and family about the doctor and therapist and how bad things are with these professional people.

The next day I received a knock on the door. I answered the door, and I saw the Butland policeman. I asked what I could do for him; the officer said, " Are you, Vincent D'Angelo? I said yes. My mother would be standing at the top of the stairs listening. The officer said that we needed to take you to the hospital. You are being sectioned 12; I asked what that means. It means that an official person, doctor, or therapist set up this section 12 on you for the reason of hurting yourself or someone else. If I didn't want to go, what would happen to me? You will be put under protective custody and go to the hospital with offices guarding you. You should come on your own. I asked what the name was on these papers; there are two names, Fay Pain and Dr. Kill Ph.D. I said I had never seen Dr. Kill. I would be escorted by the police to an ambulance and then taken to the hospital in Weymouth. When I was in the ambulance, I started to think, then started to get mad with this major problem from professional doctors who lied about section 12. When the ambulance got to the hospital, the hospital would call for security guards to guard me. When security guards put me in a room to be observed by the doctors and nurses, this would only bring out more anger within my mind, but I had to act in responsible ways outside my body. I wasn't going to feed into their dirty tactics so that I would behave myself, but I was distraught with all of these new problems from Fay Pain. Meanwhile, my mother would come to the hospital in her car and call my brothers and sister. My mother would explain that the therapist section 12 me to my brothers and sister. They couldn't believe what had happened from seeking help for stress-related problems.

When the doctor came to talk with me about 8 hours later, he would ask if I would hurt myself or anyone; I said no, doctor. The doctor asked why I was so upset right now; I said I was set up for failure with this issue. The doctor said what do you mean? I said that I was seeing a therapist Fay Pain and she was telling me that she was going to section 12 because the computer was saying that I wasn't getting better. The doctor said are you sure she said this? I said yes; I also have two cases against Butland's town, which is why I'm seeing a therapist for stress-related issues only. I said I have all the stress problems of IBS, fibromyalgia, anxiety, my body is always in pain, etc. The officers, doctors, and nurses all said that you don't look like a person who will hurt themselves or others. I asked for the doctor's opinion if I was going to hurt anyone; the doctor said no, you don't have the characteristics of that kind of person. If this therapist were only going by a computer and not her evaluation, there would be a major problem with the therapist's office. Do you know of this Dr. Kill, Ph.D.? I said no, never seen her. Well, in my opinion, other than you being upset because of the lies of section 12, I, as the attending doctor and other medical staff, find you are medically acceptable without any mental problems of hurting people or yourself. This therapist should be reported to the authorities; the doctor said, " Do you have an attorney? I said yes, you should call him to tell him what happened here and that you are medically clear from these allegations.

I would leave the hospital with my mother, talking about this new problem in the car. When we got home, my brothers and sister were there, and they asked what had happened. I said that the Butland police picked me up for a section 12. Joseph asked who started this issue; My therapist and Ph.D. doctor said I didn't know or had never seen her. Anthony would say this is medical neglect from a therapist and this unknown doctor. My mother said that this is all over the town of Butland and their dirty ways. I blame the town of Butland for these problems and the other doctors and attorneys. Plus, misleading the judges with these cases. My sister Sarah said you need to report this to law enforcement, the AG office, Norfolk, the DA office of Norfolk County, and news reporters. I said I tried this route with no results. These problems only break down my trust in this world and professional people. Even the doctor at the hospital said that I needed to report this, plus the cop here in Butland said the same thing. Joseph said that professional people notice something is wrong here and are doing nothing to help you in any way, shape, or form; that's crazy. Sarah would say, that even when you have people noticing the mistakes of other professional people they don't step forward to report or complain about the treatment of you going through all of these problems. Anthony asked if I was going to call Attorney Allen. I said yes, tomorrow. It's too late now.

I would call attorney Allen the next day for an appointment. We greeted each other, and then I explained to Dr. Lori, therapist Fay, and the Butland police with a section 12 at the hospital. Then Allen said I don't believe it. I don't know why this is happening to you, but we will find out why. (The sad part is that Allen never took the time to understand or look into why things were happening to me and my cases medically and legally) . Allen said that I needed the records from the hospital, and I'll get the records from the therapist. Will you be going back to therapist Fay? I said no way; she betrayed me, violated my rights, and had many other issues. Allen said I don't blame you, but we need someone to speak on your behalf with medical records. I said that there must be another way for independent doctors with the cases. Allen said we could get an independent doctor, but the cost is expensive, and I will need more of a retainer. I asked how much more, and Allen said $10,000.00. I said OK; I wrote out a check for $10,000.00. I said that this doctor needs to understand fibromyalgia and stress-related problems. Allen said, don't worry, I will take care of this with the independent doctor. Allen said that we need the independent doctor to piece this puzzle of your medical records together to make a stronger case with both cases. Allen said give me a couple of days, and I will call you with the information for the doctors. Allen would get back to me by e-mail with the information about the doctors. Allen would have three doctors. The first doctor cost $20,000.00 with a creditability for a doctor, this doctor I had to visit in person for evaluation. The second doctor cost $15,000.00, and with creditability, this doctor needed an evaluation. The third doctor was Allen's friend who had worked together in the past; this doctor was only charging $3,000.00 to look over the records and make decisions with my records without seeing you in person, Vincent. The other doctors want to evaluate you in person. That's why the money is high on these doctors. We sent a conversation back in forth between e-mails.

I would ask Allen which is the better doctor. Allen replied that the first doctor deals with fibromyalgia and stress-related problems, but you would need to go to New York two or three times to see him. Allen said that the third doctor would look over the records and give the diagnosis from the records without seeing you. Allen said he is the cheapest doctor, plus we worked together in the past. I said Allen, we will go with the third doctor Dr. Eric Grossman; how long will he take with the records. Allen said about a month. I went to get the hospital records from the Weymouth hospital and sent them to Allen. Allen sent for my records from therapist Fay and received them two weeks later.

CHAPTER 16
C.D.C.

I would start looking into medical information for my medical problems and conditions. When I began to look up the information, I came across with C.D.C. Center for Disease Control and Prevention. The C.D.C. is a government-run facility building; it's also a medical building for doctors, scientists, and disease control and prevention; this office also carries all medical information worldwide and in our country. It is an official guideline for the government, doctors, and scientists to follow with emergency and everyday treatments. This office is also an official guideline for our government with any serious emergencies within the country and around the world best example is COVID-19. When new medical issues are introduced, they go through the C.D.C. office and then they pass along to medical doctors all over the country. The C.D.C. will investigate the new medical issue or problem and conclude new medical issues or problems. I would find all my information on the C.D.C. website about fibromyalgia, IBS, stress-related problems, etc. When I was reading this information, I would make copies of the pages from the website. Then I would pass this information on to attorney Allen and all of my doctors. What happens from here forward is just an unbelievable nightmare; this would affect my whole life, health, and cases.

When I looked up stress-related issues, people over 50 years old are susceptible to heart attacks and strokes. Stress has physical and mental responses to the body. Physical; aches and pains, chest pain, exhaustion or trouble sleeping, headaches with dizziness or shaking, high blood pressure, muscle tension or jaw clenching, stomach or digestive problems, trouble having sex, and weak immune system. Stress can lead to emotional and mental systems like; anxiety or irritability, depression, panic attacks, and sadness with mental confusion. When people try to fix things on their own, this leads to; drinking too much, gambling, overeating or developing an eating disorder, compulsive sex or excess shopping or internet browsing, smoking more often, and using drugs. Other symptoms also assist with their side effects like fibromyalgia and IBS with similar conditions to stress. Still, when combined with all of the health conditions, fibromyalgia, IBS, and stress will have a witch's brew that is unforgiven to all patients, including me. All and any medicine has very little help with these problems, or the medicine can turn into a drug addict, who has a bad ending for the patients on either side of the problem. I also know that a nervous system problem or chemical change in the mind and body can lead to another bad ending like suicide. All the pain alone would be enough for suicide, especially when you add up stress from people in an everyday situation for seven years.

Irritable Bowel Syndrome, otherwise known as IBS. Symptoms include abdominal pain, bloating, diarrhea, and constipation, with many more symptoms in the present and future. A way a doctor explains my IBS problems is your intestines are contracting back and forth inside the abdominal part of your body. With each time these conditions happen, you could be constipation or diarrhea. Between the contractions when you have diarrhea and finally relieve yourself, it happens in your pants or running to the toilet anywhere or anytime. No matter how it happens, it's always embarrassing when you run or disappear or if you have an accident in your pants. Your nervous system has a lot to do with IBS problems when abnormalities in the nerves in your digestive system may cause you to experience more significant than average discomfort when your abdomen stretches from gas or stool. In addition, poorly coordinated signals between the brain and the intestines can cause your body to overreact to changes that generally occur in the digestive process, resulting in pain, diarrhea, or constipation.

Once the stress started, the IBS followed, and then fibromyalgia took over my life and left me helpless in this world. I try to notify the proper authorities' doctors, attorneys, law enforcement, judges, and the leaders of this state, counties, and U.S. federal authorities about the criminal actions from Robert to the town and up to senators with no results or answers. These problems would only make the conditions of stress, IBS, and fibromyalgia worse than ever before. The information for fibromyalgia from the C.D.C. website; fibromyalgia is a disorder characterized by widespread musculoskeletal pain accompanied by fatigue, sleep disorder, memory, and mood issues. Researchers believe that fibromyalgia amplifies painful sensations by affecting how your brain and spinal cord process painful and nonpainful signals. Some symptoms often begin after an event, such as physical trauma or psychological trauma, surgery, infection, or significant psychological stress. In other cases, symptoms gradually accumulate over time with no single triggering event. Many fibromyalgia people also have tension headaches, temporomandibular joint disorder, irritable bowel syndrome, anxiety, and depression. There is no cure for fibromyalgia or IBS. Some medicines can be given but with a good chance of being dependent on medication for life.

The primary symptoms of fibromyalgia include:

Widespread pain; the pain associated with fibromyalgia often is described as a constant dull ache that has lasted for at least three months. The pain must occur on both sides of your body and above and below your waist to be considered widespread.

Fatigue; people with fibromyalgia often awaken tired, even though they report sleeping for long periods of time. Sleep is often disrupted by pain, and many patients with fibromyalgia have other sleep disorders, such as restless legs syndrome and sleep apnea.

Cognitive difficulties, a symptom commonly referred to as "fibro fog," impair the ability to focus, pay attention, and concentrate on mental tasks.

Fibromyalgia often co-exists with other conditions, such as; irritable bowel syndrome, chronic fatigue syndrome, migraine and different types of headaches, interstitial cystitis or painful bladder syndrome, temporomandibular joint disorder, anxiety, depression, postural tachycardia syndrome. Many researchers believe that repeated nerve stimulation causes people with fibromyalgia's brain and spinal cord to change. This change involves an abnormal increase in certain chemicals in the brain that signal pain. In addition, the brain's pain receptors seem to develop a sort of memory of the pain and become sensitized, meaning they overreact to painful and nonpainful signals. However, doctors and researchers don't know the long-term effects and other related problems.

The C.D.C. website gave me all this information about my health issues and problems. It also could resolve my medical and legal problems, or so I thought. When I approached my attorney, doctors, and finally, the judges, I would receive the worst gratitude from these people. I did something wrong with all the hard work and information on my medical health and legal status. I proved that I was a brilliant man and took the time to look up all the information without any assistance from doctors, attorneys, or judges. Remember, all these professional people had four-plus years in college, and I outshine all of them with my knowledge and information medical and legal. I would have a problem all my life because I would take the time and effort to know all I could about my carpentry, truck driving, medical, legal, and just about everything in the world. The people I dealt with would never like a man more intelligent than themselves; I was a danger to them because I was the better man and more intelligent on the job.

The first person was my attorney Allen whom I would see. I would ask for an appointment with Allen. On the appointment day, I always had a family member with me. When I saw Allen, we greeted each other, and I started to explain all of the work I did for medical and legal reasons. Then I began to show him the files of papers that I had, and Allen would look at the documents; then, he explained that this meant nothing to the legal side of the cases. My family member and I dropped our mouths and couldn't believe it; I said, what are you talking about, Allen? It's all laid out for you as my attorney and the doctors. Allen said maybe for the doctors but not for me; I explained to you that only the doctors could give me the medical records and information, not from you.

Allen said that the perfect example the independent Dr. Eric Grossman gave is a report. It's in favor of you; plus, we had a conversation on the phone about the cases, and Dr. Eric said that he doesn't believe that the doctors in Rhode Island are not cooperating with you, Allen, or the courts, and the laws of this country. Dr. Eric said that is unheard of by a doctor or anyone acting this way. Allen said you could have a copy of Dr. Eric's report, and I will turn these papers in to the courts. I said OK, Allen, but you didn't answer the questions about the work and information that I did for us. Allen said yes, I did; I can't receive any information from you, only from doctors; I said that this came from the C.D.C. website, not from me; you can retrieve this information yourself from the website. I thought about what Allen said and asked what about you doing your investigation and discovery?

Allen would say that I am making that discovery and getting the information. I said, " Well, where are the papers on your investigation and discovery of your work with my cases? Allen would avoid and talk around in the endless circle and avoid my questions, then Allen said that I need tangible evidence and only what I can prove in a courtroom. I then asked Allen, have you put up an argument with town and town attorneys' information? Once again, the circle talk came out with no answers and no results. The problems show that Allen is not doing his job right at all. I see a breach of contract with the attorney to the client. I told Allen that I was getting better with my mind and body; I looked up more information and talked to another attorney for advice. Allen would listen without any replying. Then, I would start challenging Allen and anyone else who would lie about me or information relating to these cases.

I would have an appointment with Dr. Peter. I would bring the records I collected from the internet, C.D.C., and other places for these doctors. When I saw Dr. Peter, I showed him the folder, and he looked through them and then explained what he would like me to do with these papers. I said, for a start, you have a report from Dr. Eric stating that I'm disabled from all of my health conditions. I don't take reports from other doctors; I make my conclusion. I said this is information that you should have about my health conditions. Dr. Peter said that I have the information from the doctors within the hospital system that I belong to and the other doctors. I said, "So only information from your hospital system," which sounds like

I'm being set up for failure by your hospital system and the doctors. I said OK, then why haven't you complied with my attorney and the other doctors.

Dr. Peter said that your attorney hadn't requested records from me after the first time at the beginning of the cases. I did ask Dr. Peter when that was. Dr. Peter said about three years ago. I said attorney Allen hadn't requested updated records from you recently. Dr. Peter said no. I said OK, what about my other doctors? The documents and data are in the computer system, and if they ignore them or disregard the records, that is a problem for you to handle. I then said OK, why don't you write up the diagnosis and prognosis information for me about my health conditions. Dr. Peter said that you need to have your attorney ask for this information. I said you and I are here now, and you can write up this information, and I will pass the information on to my attorney. Dr. Peter said no, I couldn't do that; go through your attorney. You refuse your patient's medical records and no help for these cases. Dr. Peter said we were done, and he walked out of the room. When the doctor left the room, my family member and I walked out of his office. We would have all types of questions about the doctor's explanation. We would tell each other what was going on with all these professional doctors. And people who were not doing their job correctly and not helping your attorney or you with a medical and legal case.

CHAPTER 17
Social Security

It was time to visit Dr. Lori, and I will have the report from Dr. Eric. Like always, I would have somebody with me if I needed to prove anything in court. Dr. Lori would come into the room and ask how I was doing, I said pretty bad with my health, but I had news from a Dr. Eric, who evaluated my records and outcome with a disability. Dr. Lori said I make my evaluations; I don't follow other doctors' information. I said OK. If Dr. Peter said I was disabled, would you fight this issue? Dr. Lori said yes, I would. I'm your primary doctor; I am the only one who approves or denies your health with medical and legal records. So that means you are admitting you are hurting me and my cases, medical and legal. You are also ignoring outside facts of another doctor within your hospital system or outside with independent doctors. Dr. Lori said Yes, I don't care about other information from other doctors. Once again, my family members and I were astonished at what we heard from Dr. Lori's mouth. Dr. Lori would turn around and walk out of the office, saying we were all done. Dr. Lori didn't even address or examine me for health reasons I had the appointment that day.

I would return home and talk to my family about the doctors and attorneys again. The family would be disbelieved with all the information about these professional people. All of my family couldn't understand why this was happening to me. These professional people with legal authority ignored the letters I wrote and reported these actions from these professional people. I said we need to get more complex with all of these problems and address them on any legal level and by the laws of this country. The television news only shows a person with mental problems who goes on a rampage and goes crazy, hurting people for no reason. The news media and police don't show the beginning of the problems, why these problems started, or explanations. The problems should never have escalated, only if the doctors had heard the person cry for help. If it is anything like what I'm going through now, I understand that person's problems on television news that went crazy. I don't believe in crimes or violence; I do believe in getting help, but when authorities don't help, you are the loser all the way around. I have too much to lose with my cases if I did anything wrong in public or private, and I'm not going to jail for the wrong reasons. My family said that you are doing the right thing by reporting to law enforcement and anyone who will listen. Still, the problem is that nobody wants to hear the truth about their dirty systems of law, medicine, politics, and politicians with much more than is wrong with our world. Professional people are breaking the laws of our country and getting away with doing so. These laws are introduced by politicians and law enforcement and to the public. Then government people will break or manipulate the laws to fit their crimes so that they don't have to go to jail or pay for the dirty deeds that they commit.

I would retreat to my music, which helps me in many different ways. The music that I would listen to would give me some relaxation; it would help me think, help my emotions, provide me with energy when I was down, and much more. Another way of helping my mind was to play mind games on iPhones like crossword puzzles, spelling games, math games, and anything that would make me think for the better. The games would take me away from the issues of the cases and give me a break from my health and legal problems. It's no different from the movie "What Happens to Bob," with Richard Dreyfuss and Bill Murry saying take a vacation from your problems. I would do something like that but would be with music and mind puzzle games. I would not do drugs, no alcohol, no gambling, or anything that would hurt me, my people, or the laws. The most important thing to me was to figure out how to fix and prove my cases to the proper authorities and people. I would get away with my girlfriend Lisa for dinner or a movie and spend time with her. I would also try to do things around the house like cleaning, cooking, food shopping, taking showers, cutting grass, or shoveling snow, but as time went on with my illnesses, I found out that I was having a more difficult time doing these everyday things. My days of having fun are over; now, it's only doing things at a slow pace and being very smart to outwit these professional people and report them for justice.

Attorney Allen explained to me about applying to social security for some kind of income. I said that applying would interfere with the cases. Allen said no, what will happen depends on SSI benefits example, if you received $500.00 a week from your job and SSI paid $500.00 a month, you would only lose one week from your job. I asked Allen why I would make it easier for the town to pay less to me when it came to paying me every week. I asked why should the federal government have to pay for the problem that the town caused. Allen said that's what you should do for income. I said that SSI has rules with the money they give me; 1st rule is a limit on your bank accounts. 2nd rule would be when I settle the cases; my benefits will stop with SSI until the settlement money is gone, and then you need receipts of proof of where the money went. Anything that you buy with settlement money and SSI doesn't approve of the expense, or if you spend money the wrong way, SSI won't allow you to receive your benefits back to you. I said this is a lose-lose situation, and I'm afraid I have to disagree. Allen said if you get SSI benefits, you have a better chance of winning the cases. Then I asked what about the doctors not cooperating with you and why they would cooperate with SSI benefits. Allen said I was just trying to give other answers to your problems. I said fine!!!, I will apply to the SSI office, and we will see what will happen with SSI.

I would go to the Social Security office and apply. The person I was talking to said that this would take about three months to hear anything to start. If, for some reason, we deny you, there will be an appeal you can file in this office. The next step will be going in front of a judge in Sealand, RI. The next step will be an appeal to the SSI Administrative office in Washington D.C... The last step is the superior court. I started the process of waiting for answers from the Social Security office. Three months later, I was denied; I would need to go to the office and file a 2nd appeal. The person who did my appeal said that we would see if the doctors changed your status on your health. I said to the SSI worker that the doctors aren't cooperating with SSI, and the SSI worker said that's what it looks like no cooperation. The worker started to speak again; if not on the second appeal, then you'll need to go to the Sealand office and see a judge. Once again, I was denied SSI benefits and had to go to the Brock office to file papers to see the judge in the Sealand office.

The day came for the SSI court session with Judge Tony Hare; this would be the third appeal with SSI, and I was alone this time without a family member. I had to check in and prove who I was and that I had an appointment with the judge. I have never been here before, and this was a challenge for me with all my health issues. The anxiety was the first to hit me; I was so nervous being here at the SSI office. When they called to go in front of Judge Tony Hare, my anxiety kicked into high gear, then my stomach started to cramp up, and the pain from fibromyalgia was killing me. The clerk was the one who came and got me, and she explained that you have a good judge in the SSI office. The clerk asked if I had the records of the SSI office that were sent to you. I said yes, but it was on a disc, and I couldn't open it. She said, OK, I will print out the paperwork for you. OK, I saw how big my folder was at the Brock office. I went in front of the judge in Sealand, and he introduced himself as Judge Tony Hare and explained all of the court's procedures.

Judge Tony asked whether I had an attorney, and I said no. The judge said OK, I will call for an independent job adviser to help with the decision with the job aspect of the decision, and I will make sure of the legal side of the case. The judge would call this person and explain the case to her. The judge explained to her questions related to my health problems. The judge said that this man has anxiety, IBS, fibromyalgia, and a lot of stress-related problems. Can Vincent go to work, but the adviser said no. Then the judge asked if I was capable of working. The adviser said no, not with all these medical problems. The judge asked if the man could stand, sit walk, or with any kind of work. The adviser said that I couldn't work under any conditions you explained to me, Judge Tony. The adviser added that it would only worsen with him and the company if he had problems here. The adviser also said that the company's insurance would have a problem with all of his illnesses. Judge Tony said to thank her, ended the call, and told me I would notify you in the mail with a decision. The decision will take about three months.

Every time I received information, I would pass it on to attorney Allen, I would pass it through e-mail or fax, so I could prove that I sent these papers. Allen knew about my application to SSI and the bad results of being denied from my claim with SSI. After four months, I received an SSI notice in the mail; I opened the envelope and read the letter's contents, and once again, I was denied again for the third time. The judge explained that I could work at three different types of jobs. These jobs weren't in the area of Sealand or Rhode Island. The next step was Washington D.C. I would fill out the papers and send them to Washington, D.C. This step would take about one year for answers. Meanwhile, I would call attorney Allen and explain that I was denied again. The judge heard the job adviser lady clarify that I was not returning to work; three different times and added that no insurance would accept me working with my illnesses; she said this to the judge. Finally, Allen said to do the next step and see what happens. I told Allen that the medical information and records weren't clear enough for the judges or people involved in this case to make a proper decision.

We need more detailed information to prove and show how bad things are with my medical and health. I said the doctors are holding out on the exact detailed information that can explain how bad things will get with my health now and over time. These are details papers I showed you in your office, and you denied them. Since I can't do anything for you, this is the SSI office making these decisions that have nothing to do with me but with the doctors. I said that I'm letting you know why things are wrong with my cases with you, and you deny the detailed information to enter the cases that you have. I don't care about SSI; I told you that it only helps the town get off easier from their responsibilities with the value of the cases. Allen said these papers you gave me would never enter my records or any court records. I said I'm standing alone Allen, and I would ensure that the research information would get to Allen and the right people. Allen said I got to go and hung up the phone. I would notice Allen was piss-off with me going above his head for justice.

Time would pass, and I received the notice from Washington D.C., and I would read the contexts. This judge would explain that the doctors don't have details information about my diagnosis and prognosis of this case. The judge said I could only deny the claim for these reasons; without all the proper papers, I needed to decide to deny the claim; this was a waste of everybody's time with SSI cases without the appropriate paperwork from the doctors. Once again, I called Allen and explained through an e-mail the information from the SSI of denial. Allen would say the same thing, not my problem. I said Allen, you need the medical details with these cases, or we will lose both cases. Allen would only say I got to go. Later that day, I received an e-mail from Allen saying that depositions would start for the discrimination case. The 1st one will be at the office of Gram Stoneman. We will go second at the Holiday Inn in Mansfield. I would e-mail Allen back and ask about our witnesses, but I never received an e-mail back from my witnesses. I was fighting a losing battle with doctors, attorneys, witnesses, cover-ups, and soon-to-be judges. Plus, the letters that I was writing to the legal authorities complaining about the crimes that professional people were doing wrong to me, my cases, and the laws of this country.

Dark Justice White Collar Crimes

CHAPTER 18
Deposition

September 24, 2018, was the date for the first deposition at the B.F.Y. law office in Sealand, RI. The meeting was to start at 9.00 AM. Attorney Allen was late for this meeting, especially when he told me to be early for this meeting. Attorney Allen never took the time to prep me for this meeting, like other attorneys who would prep their clients. I would show up with a family member for support because I wouldn't drive under my illnesses. I would tell my brother that I was nervous and had never done anything like this. Then anxiety and stress problems would be the next start of my illnesses at this B.F.Y. attorney's office. I would also worry that attorney Allen wasn't here, which only brought out my anxiety and stress. When attorney Allen did arrive, it was half an hour late or longer. I said to Allen why are you late. Allen used the excuse of the trains and buses. I said Well, you needed to catch early trains and buses to be here on time. Allen would only ignore me and then say, " Let me check in; I said what about you prepping me for this meeting.

Allen would say it's too late now. I said this is way too late, Allen; this should have been done yesterday; Allen didn't say anything.

The meeting would start with these people in this meeting; Amy Bosh - a shorthand reporter for the commonwealth of Rhode Island; Gram Stoneman - town discrimination attorney; Allen Moakley – plaintiff (my) attorney; and then plaintiff Vincent D Angelo. Attorney Gram would have control of this meeting, and Attorney Allen would only be able to object to Attorney Gram's questions; otherwise, Allen would be quiet during these depositions. Gram asked to prove who I was; with a driver's license, then proceeded to ask where I lived, and then backtracked to information from my history up to the present time. Gram then would ask Allen if you have these records; Allen would reply, " I don't have my complete file on the case. Gram would ask me whether I had all of my licenses; I said that I gave Allen all of the copies of my licenses. Gram asked Allen do you have these copies of Vincent's licenses; Allen said no, I don't. Gram asked me what I explained about my licenses. I said I had a CDL class A driver's license, a 2A hoisting license, an HVAC license, and I had a construction license. These questions would go on forever with no meaning in my mind. Once Gram established who I was, Gram asked this other kind of ridiculous question to an ordinary citizen. The problem of the law in any way, shape, or form is asking common citizens questions of legal status who don't understand the meaning of these legal questions. The politicians and other legal figures made these laws, and understanding laws is so complicated for an ordinary person or citizen that it is a shame on the legal system and the legal figures. An ordinary person or citizen could be tricked into lies without even knowing about it by legal authorities. When this deposition was happening, I also noticed that this was a one-way track without my attorney or judge questioning or cross-questioning my questions from Gram. I would ask for a break to complain about this deposition and talk to Allen for better results if possible. Allen said that this is how judges rule out insignificant cases and save citizens' tax money. I said that this is related to the town of Butland first, not to the tax people, Allen. I said that's a lie from the judges to the politicians when they waste money for everything else in our country.

Gram said we could you this room here that we were in, and we would leave. I asked Allen why he didn't have my file like other attorneys would for their clients and themselves. Allen would say he forgot the file, and I said I trust you with my life and the money that I gave you, and this is how you take care of my case and me. I told Allen it is common to have your clients' complete records. I said that two questions from Gram are asking you, Allen, if you have any records of the case with you, and you don't even have the correct answers of yes, I have the records. That's unbelievable. I said you are an incompetent man with this whole case, Allen. I asked if the town paying you to fail this case. Allen didn't answer that question. I said how much more we will miss because you don't have my records. As I talked to Allen, I was also thinking of the following questions for Allen.

I said that this deposition was a joke and Gram has control, and there is no judge to see the actions of this attorney, Gram; all a judge will notice are words on a piece of paper that have no meaning. I don't even understand how a judge can get pertinent information and decisions from documents like these . Without the physical interaction in a courtroom, what good are these papers for when Gram is picking questions that are only set against me and without a judge and my attorney having your own opinions or questions. The documents don't show badgering, improper questions, attorneys' demeanor with witnesses or me, etc. Plus, you don't have the records, and you didn't stop this deposition, or neither did Gram. Because of no records, this could lead to malpractice on both behalf of the attorneys. Allen would avoid it as much as possible, and he didn't take the hint of stopping this deposition because he wasn't prepared with the proper records for this case. I said Allen, you haven't done your job right or advised me right in a correct way from the start. I also said that Gram knows that you are an incompetent attorney or you have been paid off and do not have your records here, and he has the edge over us now. I told Allen I needed ten minutes to calm myself to continue with these wrong procedures with my rights. Allen would leave me alone, and then, ten minutes later, we all started with more questions again.

The next question was about being sick at the end of my employment. Gram asked if I turned in a doctor's letter to excuse you from work when I was sick. I said yes. When did you give the letter, the day of visiting my doctor? I always provide a letter from my doctors on the 1st day of seeing doctors. I saw my doctor three times before I was released from my job. When I was released from my job, there was no reason I was being released from my job. I asked why I was being released, and Robert wouldn't answer. Gram asked if I remembered what that doctor's letter said; I said that my attorney had that information, and attorney Allen should have passed this information to you. There was no response from Gram because Allen didn't have my case records. I said to Gram that you are asking all of these questions and what is the purpose of these questions? I said that these questions should be asked in front of a judge. I said that this was a one-way conversation or interrogation, an infringement of my rights as a citizen of this country. Especially where my attorney can't ask any questions to correct your questions of manipulation, Gram said that this is the law at its best and laughed; I said the law is wrong with this one because every citizen in this country has a right to be in front of a judge and without the influence of this interrogation of manipulation to the judge through depositions.

Gram said we need to get this deposition done today. Gram then said that you claim discrimination against Robert Smith and the town. I said yes, I did. Can you explain what happens in this situation? I said that it was a Saturday afternoon working overtime, and Robert came in and used the excuse that he had some work to do in the office. Instead, he started to talk to three people. I was one of them. There was Scott Highway foreman, and another worker was Ben. Robert directed the conversation to Scott, but Ben and I were listening to the discussion. Robert asked why the workers were so upset with him over new contract problems in deliberation. Scott answered that it's your responsibility to have an agreement for the new contract; people depend on a new raise for their families and bills. Robert would say that he has nothing to do with this new contract; Scott said yes, you do because the old superintendent Ralph made sure that the new contracts were always signed and completed before the deadline of July 1. You have just about a year after the deadline, and there is still no contract signed. Robert would only push off this conversation and start a new conversation.

    Robert would start a new conversation about a man named Todd Williams. Gram asked me to explain the discrimination against Todd, Robert, and the town. Todd was a friend of mine, and he was a black man that is a good guy and a hard worker for the town. He worked about three jobs; one was part-time for the school dept. Then full-time with Butland, ZYX office in Butland, and a constable part-time. When Robert started verbally talking badly about Todd, I took offense to Robert's insults about Todd. Robert then started racially insulting Todd. I began to get offended more because I'm Sicilian and Italian and from a Mediterranean area, and I also have my own color with my skin.

Southern Italians and Sicilians have a skin color of olive to brown complexion, and when the sun does the tanning to these people, it turns a tan color to a dark brown color. Also, I am involved with a woman who is black, Indian, and other mixes. For that reason, I was insulted by Robert, with no consideration for people of color or nationalities, just ignorance from Robert. If I am considered white or have a color of some kind, why is it OK for any person or people to have a racial problem of any kind, and then people like me have to listen to these ignorant people saying these words or comments? Or complaints about racial situations. I should be able to report Robert no matter what and without any consequences to me, my job, or anything else. Because of Robert's words and ignorance, Robert should face charges of racial discrimination. I would have kept my job if these laws had worked correctly and in the right way. Instead, I lost my job because Robert lied about me and my job. Robert had said these comments about Todd, and I heard these comments from Robert; Robert could not have me work there anymore for that reason alone. Especially where there were witnesses, Scott and Ben, who heard Robert discriminate in his words. Robert would have to discredit me with work reason of releasing me somehow. Robert was a mean person to the workers and me, and with his power of being a superintendent, nobody could or would challenge his authority that works there because of the threats of losing their job at the ZYX office. I would start doing the same as the other workers and do my job until Robert started harassing me more and more and threatening my job by releasing me from my job. After this, I would start getting sick with Robert treating me in such a way; I was mentally abused by a man with power and winning his way with power without consequences or challenge from anyone in the ZYX office or outside sources.

The date of the incident was July 31st, 2014. I was getting sick with my stomach; at the time, I didn't put anything together till a later time with a therapist counselor. Gram would ask the next question why didn't you report this to someone. I said I did just explain that I wanted to keep my job just like everybody else at a ZYX office. Gram asks why you are complaining now about this problem. The way that Robert was trying to cover up his faults with me and with false allegations as a bad worker when I lost my job, I had no choice but to complain about a discriminating boss and a bully. I would turn this situation around with it being against Robert, especially where this was revenge for hearing Robert making racial comments about another worker Todd. I said that Robert was better off leaving me alone after the racial remarks, but he pushed me till I started getting sick, and after I got sick, Robert released me from my job without any reason or cause. "According to the laws of employment, you, as the employer by law, must give reasons for firing a person with reasons or cause"; Robert just broke the laws of employment and with the town of Butland. I said to Gram and Allen, does this matter to either of you with what I just explained about Robert breaking another law? The both of them just avoided the question; then I said, Well, these questions and deposition aren't about the truth; it's only about how you can cheat me out of justice with yourselves and help Robert and the town win the cases. I said with these rules stating that my attorney can't do much or say much with this side of deposition. This government fixes other unfair regulations and laws in favor of criminals like you attorneys.

Gram would continue questioning me and ask if I had written a letter. I said yes; I wrote many letters of complaint and reports and signed the letter. Gram would show this letter to me and say read this letter. I read this letter and discovered this wasn't the letter that I wrote or signed and sent out to the authorities. The letter that I was reading was a complaint from somebody within the town of Butland; who knew of my cases and was trying to help me prove that the town was wrong with the dismissal of my job and that the accusations were a lie against me and that it was in favor of the town with no signature on the paper. When Gram heard I denied this letter that he showed me, Gram got so frustrated with the information that he thought he would help win the case in his and the town's favor. Plus, a court reporter was recording. So Gram was wrong with the letter, and this wasn't a good thing for Gram or the town. Then Gram started to attack the SSI insurance office and their information about me from them. I asked Gram what this has to do with your side of the case; this doesn't show any fault between the town and me. The SSI office is an office for the assistance of medical and financial assistance. Allen would ask me to leave the office and go off the record to discuss this SSI insurance. Gram and Allen would discuss whether or not to use my information from SSI insurance. Finally, Gram would call me back and say that we would not use this SSI information. Then Gram said that we were all done with my deposition, and you were all set to go home. I said OK, but I wanted to talk to Allen before leaving.

Allen and I would leave the office and building, and I asked why they didn't do more for the case and me. I said that you copy my first attorney, Bob's information from the discrimination board. You didn't write your complaint information for this case. These cases are in two different areas: the discrimination board and the other for the US district court, and they both have different rules. I asked what would happen if the information you copied wasn't the correct information on all levels. I said that the questioning from Gram about your original paperwork to the case is all wrong; I also said this to attorney Bob, and I lost the discrimination board answer. I told Allen that you better start doing his job as an attorney, or there would be legal consequences for you; I would report you and these two cases to the authorities; I'm not afraid of a fight on any legal level or otherwise. You see how I'm fighting with doctors, Robert, the town, and town attorneys, and you can be added with no problems.

CHAPTER 19

Second Deposition

October 3, 2018, would be the date for new superintendent Jimmy Flynn and retired superintendent Robert Smith's depositions. Jimmy would be the first at 10.00 AM, and Robert would be the second at 12.48 PM for their depositions. I would show up early, and attorney Allen was nowhere to be found; again, Allen was late for his depositions, and his office was around the corner from Holiday Inn. When Allen did show up, I asked what was there to expect with today's depositions. Allen said that you would see Jimmy and Robert's depositions. I asked what happened to the list of people you asked for as witnesses on my behalf. Allen made up excuses that nobody would come forward and lose their job over you or this case, and you also don't have money for these depositions to continue. Allen would also say it's a waste of money if the town has everybody lying about you to keep their job and free the town from any wrongful doings. I said, then I'm in a losing battle without the truth for justice. Allen would explain that Jimmy would be first and then Robert. I asked why he would have Jimmy; Allen replied because he was there when you worked, and now he is the new superintendent. I said Jimmy never interacted with me other than saying hello or goodbye. Allen said we would see what his story was. Allen would say that I need to be quiet during the depositions. If not, you will be kicked out of the meeting. When you have any questions, write them down, and I'll request your questions.

Attorney Allen asked if they were ready to start the deposition. Gram said yes, we are ready. Allen started to explain the procedures of this deposition; Allen would say this is for the record we have Brenda Roth as a court reporter, Gram Stoneman attorney for defendants for the town of Butland, we also have from the town's new superintendent Jimmy Flynn, Vincent D Angelo plaintiff, and Allen Moakley attorney for the plaintiff. Allen asked if Robert would show up today to Gram; Gram said he would be here. Allen would start asking for a license for Jimmy to prove who he was for the record. Allen asks questions about Jimmy's history to the present. One of the questions was did you go to college and Jimmy said yes. Allen asked what courses he took; Jimmy said civil engineering BS degree.

Then Allen asked about how Jimmy met Vince; Jimmy said from a job interview for the town of Butland and when we hired Vince. Allen asked if you were the only one or others at the interview; Jimmy said there were three people. Allen said, " Can you identify who was there; Jimmy said there was superintendent Robert Smith and me, the other one; I don't remember his name. Allen asked, do you remember assistant supervisor Chuck Freedman? Jimmy said I don't remember. Allen asks what do you know about Vince and his job? Jimmy said that all the foremen were complaining about his performance at work. Allen asked these men's names, Moe Dirt, Moe Heap, and Jeff Knowles. Allen said that all, Jimmy? Jimmy said there are seven foremen in the ZYX office. Allen asked; what are the other four foremen? Jimmy said, I don't remember. Allen said you are the new acting superintendent; Jimmy said yes; Allen said, " Well, don't you know your men who work for you? Jimmy repeated I don't remember their names. Allen asked did you have any complaints from Robert when he was in office. I don't remember. Allen asked how reliable the foremen's stories were; Jimmy said very reliably. Allen said really, what kind of work were they complaining about with Vince. Jimmy said I don't remember.

Allen would say let me help you to remember what Vince was doing. As an assistant supervisor at the time, Allen said only four years back. When hiring new workers, where do the new workers start working, and in what department? Jimmy said that the new workers start in the sanitation department. Allen said how long before they are moved up in position; Jimmy said when a new job opens up or one year later after probation time. Allen said did a new job open up for Vince? Jimmy said no, he was only in the sanitation department. Allen said so does that mean that Vince was always on the garbage trucks with two other workers? Jimmy said yes. Allen said so; where did the foremen get involved with seeing Vince not working? Were their foremen on the garbage trucks? Jimmy said no foremen are on the garbage trucks. Allen said then, how do you know the truth of the foremen's stories? I don't remember. Allen would ask Jimmy have you witnessed anything that Vince did wrong with the ZYX office; Jimmy said I don't remember.

Allen said, " Then why are you here, were you told to lie about Vince and his job? Gram said I object to this questioning, Allen responded to Gram well; this man doesn't have any answers; it looks like someone programs him into telling these lies. Gram was quiet after that; Allen asked can I continue with my questioning, and Gram said yes. Allen said that we might need to have the seven foremen come in for depositions, and we will find out the truth then if Jimmy's statement is correct or incorrect with perjury. Gram got upset and asked for a break to talk to Jimmy; Allen said OK. So Allen and I left the room, and we had our talk about this situation; Allen said that this guy had no idea of what was going on with this questioning or his job, and whether the complaints about you were true or not true. I said that I was telling you in the notes that he was lying, and Jimmy was never around except in the morning to pass out the work orders or maybe around the workyard or office. Allen said this is good for us; I said Robert would be just as bad if not worse than Jimmy.

We would all return to the table and proceed with the questioning about Vince getting sick. Allen asked what the rules for employees getting sick are; Jimmy said they needed a doctor's letter to excuse them from work. Allen asked whether Vince provided these letters; Jimmy said yes. Allen asked if this information was in the Butland handbook; Jimmy said yes. Then, Allen asked why Vince was released from his job; Jimmy said work performance. Allen said, " What do you mean you said that he was on the back of a garbage truck throwing trash all day? Can a person make mistakes with this job? Jimmy said not really. Allen said then, how can you explain his performance; Jimmy said I can't. Allen said, once again were you sent here to lie about Vince and his job? Jimmy had no answer. Gram said I object to this questioning, Allen replied there is something wrong here to Gram. Allen said I believe that we are all set with this witness, and we can start with Robert next. Gram agreed. While waiting on Robert, Allen and I went to talk about the rest of the deposition with Jimmy. I said that I wanted to know if you believed me about the lies with all the town and the power of the town position; Allen said that something is going on with this town of Butland, but we have no proof. I said that there is proof with all the complaints that just vanishes. Allen said that we need to get back to Robert's deposition.

October 3, 2018, the time was 12.38 PM, and Robert was the second witness in this case between Vincent D Angelo, plaintiff, and Robert Smith, defendant, and the town of Butland, defendant. First, Allen would go through the procedures of introductions of the case and ask for a license from Robert to prove who he was. Then, Allen started asking questions to Robert; Allen asked Robert what high school did you go to, and Robert said Butland High and graduated in 1969. Allen said did you go to college? Robert said no college; I started with the Butland ZYX office right out of high school. Allen said, " How long have you been at the ZYX office, Robert said from 1969 to 2015, then I retired. Allen asks Robert what were your reasons for retiring? Robert said my health was failing. Allen asked would there be another reason. Robert said no with an attitude. Next, Allen asked what position did you start? Robert said at the end of his retirement; I was a superintendent; Robert said when he started, I was a laborer, truck driver, heavy equipment operator, foreman, assistant supervisor, and final superintendent. Allen said that you actually grew up with the ZYX office and then grew with power as a superintendent and spent all of your life in Butland; Robert said yes. Next, Allen asks if Robert had any problems or complaints about him being at all his jobs with the ZYX office. Robert said no; Allen said that if I look up your record with the ZYX office will I find any problems or complaints from other people against you? Robert said no, I never had any problems or complaints with my job. Allen said that if you are lying, this would be perjury for the record. Robert said I understand, but no problems or complaints.

Allen asks how do you know Vince; Robert explains that he was a subcontractor for snowplowing. Allen said, " Do you remember how long this job with Vince; Robert would say no, sure, maybe ten years before I hired him for full-time employment with the town. Allen said let me help you with your memory. Do you remember a day back in 2002, a brand-new blue pick-up F-250 series with an 8ft. plow blade? Robert said no. Allen asked what the requirements are for plowing; Robert said I wanted 250 trucks or bigger with an 8ft plow or bigger. Allen said OK, you don't remember when Vince came in and asked for two separate applications. One was for plowing, and the other was for full-time employment with the town. Robert said no. Allen asked do you remembered a conversation with Vince about a new truck and working the streets and that Vince would destroy his brand-new truck on the streets of Butland, Robert said no, I don't remember. Allen said when a new contractor asks for a plowing position, don't you check and see if the trucks check out for your requirements. Robert said no. Allen said OK do you remember a man asking for two applications, Robert said no. Allen asked what made you hire Vince as a town employee, Robert said he was an excellent snowplow driver, and I thought he would be a plus for the ZYX office. Allen said that Vince was a good worker, then what changed the fact of Vince being a bad worker? Robert said I don't know.

    Allen said you are the superintendent who doesn't know everything under your office's leadership. Robert said that I rely on the assistant supervisors and the foremen to relay the information. Allen asked what happens when your leaders lie about things or don't know; Robert said I don't know myself. Allen said, " How do you know that Vince was a bad worker, Robert said through my leaders. Allen said Well do you check up on people and make sure that the information is correct, Robert said no, I believe in my leaders. Allen said there could be a lie with your leaders or a lie with you being in charge as a superintendent, Robert said it could happen, but I trust my leaders and myself. Allen asked about Vince's job from the beginning of the hire, Robert said that he was hired as a laborer and truck driver, and Vince was placed with the sanitation department. Allen asks Robert did Vince's job changed before his dismissal. Robert said no, he was still in the sanitation department. Allen said, then how could he foul his job throwing trash all day? Robert said I don't know. Allen said once again; you're the boss of this office; don't you have control over everything? Robert said no. Gram said I object. Allen said to Gram that this was a joke; the man didn't know anything about his own office or the leaders or workers. Gram said we need a break. Allen said OK.

Allen said we would leave the room so you could talk to your client. Allen and I left the room, and we started talking about Robert's deposition. Allen said that Robert didn't know what happened in his office and that he was lying about all the questions. Allen said Robert or Jimmy never took the time to check things out to be sure of the truth if any issues are about you, Vince. Allen said it sounds like they are making up the story with lies. I told Allen that we needed to have a courtroom status to hear other witnesses from the town workers, which would not cost me any money. I said they were both lying about their stories with the notes I would be passing you. Plus, with your questioning about specific questions to Jimmy, you nail him with his lies, and then Robert playing the remembering game, you know they are both lying about the whole story. I said that this is perjury with these court record recordings; we should be able to use the court records recording against Robert, Jimmy, the town, and the town attorney. Allen said you are getting too far ahead of yourself. We need to finish here first; then, we can look at these other problems when receiving the transcripts. I said to Allen what about the witnesses I gave you? Allen, Allen said I told you early that nobody will come forward for you and jeopardize their job, and you are running out of money. Allen said we needed to get back to the meeting. As Allen and I went back to the room, I started to think about Allen's statement about the money and whether he was trying to get more money from me. I would have another problem that I would think about, and with all the problems that Allen has caused my family and me.

We all returned to the deposition table, and Allen started to ask questions to Robert. Allen said when you interviewed Vince did you have a private conversation about Vince being your eyes, ears, and a stoolie on the men at the ZYX office? Robert said I don't remember. Allen said, " Did you ever say to Vince that he could trust you and the men you couldn't trust? Again, Robert said, " I don't remember. Allen said they are a particular way of throwing the trash or standards for removing it; Robert said no. Allen then explained how Vince didn't do his job correctly; Robert said, I don't know. Allen said what do you mean you don't know? Allen said that you are the boss and you depend on other leaders to give you a proper answer on Vince, and you don't check out the truth to the stories, and then you destroyed a man's living with I don't know. Robert said I did nothing of the kind. Gram then jumped in and said, I object. Allen said Robert was lying about his story, and also Jimmy was lying; this was a hoax, a joke of the law system and the town's power and money to waste. Gram said that Robert has a memory issue and his medications. Allen said that this was not an excuse. You have a man hanging in the balance of the loss of his job, financial problems, and most importantly, his health problems from this job, and Robert's complaints with lies.

Gram said Well, your client should not have screwed up his job with the town of Butland. Allen then said Well, I think we are done with this deposition, and then Allen closed the meeting with the court reporter. I asked Allen if we could talk more about the deposition; Allen said yes, we can. I asked Allen for his opinion; Allen said it looked good for us. Robert and Jimmy didn't know anything about their job or everyday operations or even the accusations against you. I asked Allen what would happen now;

Allen said we would have to wait for 3 to 4 months for a court date with the judge. I said OK, Allen, so we are done with this part of the case, Allen said yes. Allen said I would keep in touch with you about Workmen's Comp. Case.

CHAPTER 20
Family & White Collar Crimes

I would leave Allen after the depositions along with Robert and Gram. My anxiety during the depositions would only increase after the depositions. Allen did a good job questioning Robert and Jimmy and brought out many good points of view with his questioning. As I was driving home and thinking about Allen and depositions, I would start feeling the anxiety taking over my body. My mind would also begin to wonder if we did a good enough job that show the proper proof for a judge to rule in our favor. I started having a hard time trying to get home. I had difficulty driving because of the anxiety attacks that were getting stronger and the pain. I eventually got home, and my mother asked what happened with the depositions. I said to my mother I was having an anxiety attack. I need time to calm down first; I want you to call my brothers and sister to come over, and I will explain everything together.

My family would come over to the house, and we all sat around the table. I would explain the depositions and how Allen brought out good questions about my job; and how I was dismissed from my job without a proper reason and without checking any facts of their stories from the foremen, assistant supervisor, and superintendent. Town attorney Gram objects to a lot of questions from Allen. The witnesses, Jimmy and Robert, showed that they were lying about their stories and questioning in such a way; Allen was asking these questions. Allen accused them of lying, and Gram objected and protected his clients. During the questioning, I believed that Allen and I were getting to the truth from Jimmy and Robert; and that they were lying about everything with their stories and their facts. This would also lead to perjury from both of them, and the town attorney, plus the town, is responsible for all involvement.

I then said if anyone here had any doubts about who was at fault, it only showed the town did the wrong with Allen's questioning and my complaints from the beginning. I will receive the transcripts, and then you can read them for yourselves. My brother Joseph said why did Allen give you a hard time with everything up until now? I said I don't know why, but there is a long way to go. My brother Anthony said, " Remember, who will if you don't stand up for yourself? It would help if you fought till the end of this lawsuit. When you are right with problems, you need to fight till the end. I said we need to see if Allen keeps improving himself over time or let me and the cases down for the worst. My mother would say do you feel better with the outcome of the depositions on this side? I said yes and no; it all depends on the judge allowing the case to go to court so we can prove more with more witnesses and evidence. I told my family that Allen didn't have the list of witnesses come in because I didn't have enough money to cover the expenses. My family didn't like the explanation from Allen; my mother said you have the money. The problem is we are not giving any more money to Allen.

I started thinking about how I would look up information about my health issues and problems. Now it's time to look into WHITE-COLLAR CRIMES' medical and legal laws and how they would work and affect me and my cases. Trillions of WHITE-COLLAR CRIMES started from the beginning time of men on this earth up to the present times. The doctors didn't want to write up a proper diagnosis and prognosis for my attorney or me, and the courts involved in these cases. The doctors who don't keep the authentic medical records complete are breaking laws; this would mean that a doctor should not ad-lib the medical records in any way, shape, or form and not leave medical information out in any way, shape, or form. Doctors can be neglectful in their practice for the two reasons I said before. There are many other ways for a doctor to be negligent to a patient; prescribing too much or not enough medicine, sexual abuse, and falsifying medical records, which could lead to falsifying legal records, courts, and much more. The two that apply to me are falsifying medical and legal documents and possibly many other neglect problems or broken laws from a doctor. When you have an attorney and court involvement; with the doctor, the doctor doesn't want to cooperate; this is also neglect of the responsibilities of a doctor. WHITE-COLLAR CRIMES consist of non-violent crimes that can have a major effect on people, businesses, government officials, and, most importantly, this country's laws.

When I did look up the information on WHITE-COLLOR CRIMES, I found information that goes across many different areas of the laws. First, there are acts of known criminal acts like bribery, money laundering, fraud, inside trading, embezzlement, and espionage. Then there is also corporate crime, organized transnational crime, and crimes of national interest. Then white-collar crimes run hand in hand with blue-collar crime, which is a mafia-style of crime, against businesses, government officials, attorneys, judges, police, and politicians. These two crimes work together because the white-collar criminal bosses need enforcement from the blue-collar criminals. It's no different from our law system and how the politicians make the laws and the law enforcement are the enforcers. The difference between the two is that one stands for the good of the people and our laws; the other is from criminal acts that underhanded the true meaning of criminals at their best to do wrong to this country's citizens. Also, for their greed, power, and dishonorable men. The difference between blue-collar crimes and white-collar crimes is that blue-collar crimes are the physical operation of a crime, and white-collar crime is the operation's mastermind. Both of these crimes are very dangerous, and they work hand in hand with each other. For example, our own two presidents, John F. Kennedy and Abraham Lincoln were assassinated with white-collar crimes with blue-collar crimes that followed. Both crimes are different categories; white-collar crimes are more deadly than blue-collar crimes.

White-collar crimes start with evil that can end so badly and are deadly. White-collar crimes are the brainstorm of the crimes and the downfall of leaders of corruption. The problem would start from the beginning of man's time. This is another way of how the leaders of our world got into power by destroying their rivals and competitors. These problems would plague humanity from the past to the present and in our future. Remember these words I hear every day from all the people in our world " I don't care about anything." These leaders set an example for the public and citizens of our world. These problems would also trickle down to all levels of life, especially when the children say, "I don't care about anything." The worst teachers are the adults of the world the children. The children start out innocent until the child starts to learn about the corruption from the adults and more.

The sad story of white-collar crimes is that they can happen to anyone and go undetected for the first time or over many years. One of the reasons is that white-collar has no identifying situation or pacific areas untouchable. White-collar crimes can go undetected in many ways and right in front of people without notice. Examples are; sexual harassment, a boss harassing the workers, favoritism which prevents a raise or promotion, bribery on all levels and in different ways, a higher-level white-collar crime to protect government officials when they are breaking our laws, not allowing a police report to be filed, not allowing a complaint to be filed to the police, writing letters of complaint to the politicians about the conditions of the federal or state or town or city levels. Filing complaints and letters with the attorney general office was ignored. These are only some white-collar crimes happening as I explain them today in our world. The police or law enforcement doesn't know how to handle these problems running wild throughout the streets, jobs, offices, government officials, and politicians. Let's not forget the money side of being at fault and being in the wrong by breaking the laws, lawsuits, and jail terms when found guilty. God forbid top officials to be found guilty of a crime and get sued and have to pay big money, especially if it's malicious intentions; the money is three times the value of a lawsuit.

Blue-collar crimes and criminals are the enforcers of white-collar crime leaders, but some blue-collar criminals think they are smarter than the people or the police authorities. In reality, blue-collar criminals are the dumbest people around in our world because they are the ones going to jail. The white-collar crimes are sitting in a wealthy home living large off of you, and you are going to jail with blue-collar crimes. There is so much more to explain about white-collar crimes. There are books that have been made with our laws. There are also true stories in crime books made for information like the one I'm writing. I will explain more about white-collar crimes in this story.

CHAPTER 21

Workmen's Compensation

A couple of weeks later, after the deposition, I would call attorney Allen and ask about Workmen's Comp. Case. I wanted to know when we would go over the Workmen's Comp. case information. I would also ask how long it will take to hear from the U.S. District Court. Allen would say you need to come into my office, and we can talk about the Workmen's Comp. Case. I would meet with Allen with a family member, and the first question was, what is happening with the U.S. District Court? Allen said that we have to wait for an answer from the judge for a court date. I then said my retainer with you would not be needed until we go to court; Allen said yes. OK, Allen, let's talk about the Workmen's Comp. Case. Allen said what do you want to know? I looked at Allen strangely after asking that question; I asked if you had any steps or procedures that you follow with Workmen's Comp. Case and with your clients and what are they.

Allen noticed that I was thinking better about the cases and how I was conducting myself. Then Allen asked how my health was doing. I said that I was trying to manage my anxiety and fibromyalgia, but the pain from fibromyalgia is killing me and my body. I said that the confusion from my anxiety was getting better in time. I'm thinking better, trying to socialize with people and occupy myself for the better. Allen said that's good, but we still have a problem with the doctors not coming forward with the proper diagnosis and prognosis. I said why don't we get an independent doctor to evaluate my entire medical case and the court cases. Allen said that's a good idea, but you need to pay for the evaluation. Do you have the money for this evaluation? I thought that I didn't pay for anything when it came to Workmen's Comp. Case. Allen said yes, you do pay for extras. You should explain to my doctors that you need the proper medical records to help us prove our case of Workmen's Comp. Case and overall proper information. Allen said I did ask them for the medical records and hadn't got a response from them. I said you need to argue with these doctors or take this problem to the judge and say that the doctors don't want to cooperate with a patient, attorney, judge, and court. Allen argued with me that he couldn't do that in any way, shape, or form.

I said, Allen, that you were perfect with your questions about the town deposition. And now you are playing in the opposite direction with me and these cases. I also said you should think of better ways to beat these cases with our laws. I said that you were supposed to think of an outside doctor who could evaluate this case and carry the strength of my doctors by proving my doctors were wrong with their medical information or withholding medical information. I've been telling you, Allen, that all the medical information is not complete with my doctors. Therefore, we should bring a case against my doctors for holding out medical information, which is also medical neglect and malpractice with a patient. Allen would only say that we can consider that idea later. I said you are wrong; this information and lawsuit could be used as leverage against the doctors to cooperate with you as my attorney and with the laws, judges, and courts. The law system works against criminals who don't cooperate with the police, DA attorneys, and courts. Allen said I was wrong with all of these problems and cases. My temperament started to build with Allen because I knew that the answers were wrong with how he explained the laws to my cases. I have told Allen that I have talked to other attorneys from the past and present and told Allen about my conversations in detail with these other attorneys. Then Allen looks at me and lies to my face about the same laws and information that the other attorneys warn me about with Allen as well.

I said Allen, we are going around and around. We need to look for the laws that will work for the cases. I said to Allen remember, I have spoken to other attorneys about my cases and looking for better information to win my cases for both of us together. Allen would only turn his head and ignore my words and conversation. I asked Allen if you would find the proper doctor who understands my health conditions, especially fibromyalgia problems. I said that fibromyalgia is the main problem at this point in the case, especially if my doctors are not acknowledging my medical problems. Allen would ask about the money needed for the examination issue with the independent doctor. I said I guess you are forcing me to pay for this doctor when it's your job to pay and then take it back as an expense at the end as medical expenses of the case. Allen would respond with a no for an answer; you need to pay Vince. I said that you needed to think of this when the first sign of the doctors were not cooperating with us and the cases. Allen said that we are doing this now, so it's not a big deal. I said yes, it's a big deal because we are not prepared for these cases or anything else that comes up with problems; remember that the town is lying with this whole problem and cases. I said Allen, I'm not an attorney, but I know how to be prepared for cases, and that doesn't explain your training, schooling, or experience with your office; I have no experience, but I know what to do. Allen ended this meeting and stated that I'd call you when I found a doctor for an examination. Allen would leave me hanging every time or go around and around with no answers to my questions.

A couple of weeks later, I received a phone call from Allen saying that the town was trying to dismiss the Workmen's Comp. Case. I asked Allen did you filed papers against the town for Workmen's Comp. Case, Allen said yes. I asked them why they would be able to deny the claim. Allen said they could deny the claim, and the way you've been thinking about the town lying, it is possible. Allen said that your doctors make this case harder because the doctors aren't cooperating with the laws. I noticed that Allen finally admitted that the doctors were wrong legally. But Allen still insisted that he couldn't do anything about the doctors on a legal level. I would be plagued with Allen's lies and misleading information about the laws; this would also be applied to the doctors and the proper legal authorities' offices where I made criminal reports and complaints reports. Allen said we need to go to Sealand to answer these questions with the town attorney representing Workmen's Comp. Case. Allen would receive a date to go in front of a conciliation person for Workmen's Comp. Case. Allen would pass this information forward to me. In response to Allen, I asked if I was going to this meeting. Allen said you don't have to; I wanted to be there and meet this town attorney. Allen said OK, to me come.

The day came to go to Workmen's Comp. Office in Sealand. Allen would be late for this meeting; like always, he gave an excuse to take the buses and trains into Sealand, which made him late. Allen asked me if I saw the town attorney; I said no, I don't even know who they are. Allen said I would look for her; I said it's a woman's attorney, and Allen said yes. I ask what her name is. Allen said I think it is Kerry Dunn; I said you don't know, and Allen walked away from me. Allen found Kerry, and she said that we had to wait to be called. Allen would return to explain that we were waiting for the case to be called. I ask Allen did you find out the reasons why we're here. Allen said no; I said have you talked on the phone with this attorney? Allen said yes, that's how I knew she was a woman. With your conversation with her, I said didn't you ask for reasons for being here.

Allen would be caught in a lie at this point; Allen would say it was an only acknowledgment of the attorneys and case conversation. I said so you didn't talk about the criteria of the case in any way, shape, or form, just introductions. Allen would say yes. I said I have a hard time believing this, Allen; all attorneys talk about their cases and disclose the information about their cases; it is the law, and you are obligated to explain your conversation to me; this also goes for the other case as well. There are no private conversations between attorneys, especially regarding your clients. Allen would just look at me with amazement, then say that I've been doing a lot of homework with the cases and the general laws and medical laws. I said yes, Allen; I have done a lot of reading, especially when I don't understand issues or trust people.

An office lady would call out the case name, and we all went to the door. We were taken to an office where a lady was sitting behind a desk. This lady was a conciliation official for Workmen's Comp. Office. We all sat down, and she introduced herself as Lisa White, a conciliation official for the Workmen's Comp. Office and the Commonwealth of Rhode Island. Lisa asks for introductions from the attorneys, Allen Moakley, attorney for the plaintiff Vincent D' Angelo, and Kerry Dunn for the defendant's town of Butland. Lisa asked the gentleman in the seat; I said Vincent D' Angelo, the plaintiff.

Lisa stated that this case is a question of going forward to a Workmen's Comp. Judge. Allen started. I have sent in all the paperwork and medical records. Kerry would interrupt, stating that there is no medical threshold met for requirements by laws. Lisa was bothered by Kerry's interruption and her reciting the laws. Lisa said I know the laws and the rights of the people involved with this case. Lisa said that my job is to determine whether or not to go forward to a judge and not to determine the case as a whole. If all the proper paperwork is done, it will go forward to the judge for a hearing. I agreed that all the appropriate paperwork is done right, and yes, this case will go forward to a judge after all. Lisa would then say you filed this grievance against Allen and Vincent, which wasn't true. Attorney Kerry was so upset with her decision from Lisa; that Kerry asked Allen to speak to him in private. I told Allen I wanted to hear the conversation; Allen said no, this is an attorney conversation only. I asked Allen if they would explain the conversation to me later, but Allen would only avoid the question, and I never heard any conversation information from Kerry and Allen. Like any other person, I would try to listen to the conversation between Allen and Kerry but had no luck trying to hear the conversation through the door.

When the conversation was over between the attorneys, I asked Allen to explain the discussion. Allen said that I would not explain the conversation to you. I said that you want me to believe in you, but you are giving reasons not to believe in you instead. Allen said I don't care what you believe in, Vince. Allen said that you won the decision from Lisa's conciliation official to go in front of a judge. However, you did piss off Kerry with the answer from Lisa's conciliation official. Allen said you are in a big fight with the town and this attorney, Kerry. I said Allen remember that you wanted to go after workmen's comp. case, not me at first, then I gave in to you. I asked Allen are you going to be able to handle this attorney and town lies and bull shit, Allen would say yes to my question. I asked what the next step for us was, and Allen said yes. Do we need to go over the case and prep for this case? Allen said I would let you know about that regarding a hearing date. I asked about the independent doctor, and Allen said I'm working on the doctor; I have some in mind, but I still haven't decided yet. I said it's been about two months; again, Allen would only walk away from the question, leaving me no answers.

CHAPTER 22
Judge Decision

On February 17, 2019, I received the news about the federal court judge. Allen would send me an e-mail with a decision from Federal Judge Dick Shawburg. I would print out the e-mail and start to read these papers. The paperwork explains reference cases throughout the paperwork, making things hard to understand. When I got to the end of the paperwork, I expected a court date to go to. Instead, I read that Judge Dick Shawburg made a final decision. The judge's decision was in favor of the town, and the town won the decision from the judge. Being Italian, I would get so mad, angry, hatred, I wanted to destroy the world, but I would always hold on to my feelings. When my mind went on a rampage, I would go through my feelings of being betrayed by my attorney Allen. The judge was misled by his decision by false depositions and two attorneys, Gram and Allen. I tried to calm down and get a hold of my senses. This was very difficult because I felt like I was being taken advantage of in so many ways and with health problems that hurt so bad with all the stress. I told the truth to all the people involved with my cases, and it's like nobody cared about me, my health, or the fact that multiple crimes were happening in these two cases. The laws of this country and the politicians and judges in charge of these laws let me down as a person, citizen, and human being. I would decide to put down the acknowledgment of this paperwork and buy a case of beers and drink my night away and listen to the music that helps me with health problems.

The next day I would wake up, and I would be in pain from fibromyalgia, which was a recurring problem for me and would only worsen in time. It took me about an hour to get my bearings together because of the fibromyalgia pain, dizziness, headaches, and other problems; then, I would try to read the court decision repeatedly to understand and grasp their decision. I would read these papers to understand and refresh my mind on the issues with this decision. I started to think that we were looking for a court date, not a decision from the judge. I told myself I needed to call Allen and start asking questions about what happened all around and for Allen to explain these papers and decisions. I called Allen for an appointment, and Allen said that you don't need one; I'll explain over the phone.

Allen said your case is over, and I will not do your appeal for you; I asked how it could be over when we didn't even get a chance to go in front of the judge. We were looking for a court date; what happened, Allen? The judge decided that he didn't need to waste the court's time with a nuisance case. What do you mean, Allen? I said that other witnesses and evidence would be brought into court. Allen said that the judge only used the depositions and made a judgment from the depositions. I got so upset that I told Allen that these depositions were bull shit; it's a one-way track with no return for justice. It's a way of discarding a case with very few consequences for the town responsible for their worker's mental health, physical health, and well-being. I said that people who are drug users and have alcohol problems get treated better at their job for help than a person who receives mental abuse and discrimination from their boss like me.

Allen would say that I am out of this case, and I will not represent you with an appeal. I ask why you are not representing me with an appeal, plus the facts of this being the mess and mistakes that you caused with both cases. I asked if I could see the paperwork you sent to the court; Allen said no, the courts have the paperwork, and the courts will not let you see these papers. Allen said that you have ten days to write to the judge, and then you have 30 days for an appeal and retrieve an attorney for an appeal. I ask if you will represent me with the Workmen's Comp. Case? Allen said yes. I said OK, Allen, I have about $2000.00 in the retainer money. I will be receiving all that money back, Allen. Allen said yes, you will. Allen said we have another date for the Workmen's Comp. case. I asked when. Allen said I have to get back to you when that date comes. I asked how long I had to wait for this return of my money; Allen said about two weeks. I asked Allen about the independent doctor, and Allen said I'll send you some resumes about these doctors. I said OK, Allen, we are done, and I hung up the phone with Allen. About a week later, I received a letter from Allen, and I opened the letter; I was expecting a check. Instead, it wasn't a check. It was a bill for a visit to Workmen's Comp. Case and the phone call about the judge's decision and then expenses with the depositions done in late September and early October, and now we are receiving a bill in late February. Allen has stolen about $1600.00 between all of these bills. Workmen's Comp. case is free until we settle, and the depositions were about five months ago; the only account that may be appropriate is the phone call about the judge's decision. You would think that Allen wouldn't charge me for a phone call about an explanation of the decision from the judge. Plus, Allen did not do his job as an attorney, especially when he made a mess and mistakes in the case and did not fight hard enough with the town attorney and the judge to ask for a court date for this case.

My mother would go down to Florida from October to May, and I would be home with my sister and her boyfriend. I would receive a phone call from my mother asking me how I was doing and how was the house and my sister. I said everybody was OK, mother. My mother asked how the case was going. I said we need to get all of us together, and I'll explain everything to you. Mother said to call everyone, and we went over the news. I would call Lisa, Joseph, Anthony, and Sarah for a day when we were all available. We were all set up for a Saturday, and we called up our mother to explain the judge's decision, Allen, and the money that Allen had stolen from the retainer money and his statement bill. I started with the judge. First, I explained that Allen and I were waiting for a court date; instead, the judge gave a judgment in favor of the town. I said that the judge passed out reference cases to answer how he decided without having a court session. The average citizen wouldn't understand any paperwork or judgment with all the reference cases that this judge wrote into his judgment. What is a citizen supposed to do with these reference cases? Look up all the reference cases that the average citizen doesn't have access to or has no knowledge of these books or information. Being in an Italian family, everybody got upset except Lisa. She was bothered that the law can let you down without any justice.

Meanwhile, everybody had their own opinion starting with my mother; my mother began to say that Allen let you down big time and then said people were paid off for these criminal acts. Joseph said the politicians are the real criminals, and they are the criminal's teachers to our population and the public that follows these head criminals, who are the politicians. Anthony said the politicians stopped the mafia so that they could take control and be the greedy ones only and the most powerful with all the money. Then they would destroy the small guy and lock him up in jail for the same crimes that the politicians do every day of their lives. My sister Sarah said that because the person with the idea of criminal acts is only the leader of WHITE-COLLAR CRIMES, you have the BLUE-COLLAR CRIMES FOLLOWS, AND THAT'S WHY THERE ARE CRIMINALS IN THE WORLD. The criminal world is from the president's down to the bums in the streets; nobody is safe if everybody is on the take or hurting our very system of laws, people, and humanity. I said that the politicians are like the drug dealers. There is never enough money for them, so they will take advantage of people and everything they can, including killing them.

I would continue to explain to my family; now, Allen sent me an e-mail with the decision about the judge and the case. Allen didn't even put up an argument for a court session with the judge. When I called Allen, he said that it's over with the discrimination case, and I will not appeal the matter to you; you need to find a new attorney for the appeal. When my family heard that information, the chaos started with everybody arguing about Allen leaving me in my time of legal needs, especially without going to court, and then not helping with the appeal. The family said that Allen took my money and ran away with it. Also, Allen must have gotten paid off for intentionally losing the case without a fight or argument, or he just laid down for them. I said that Allen had played a game with me, going back and forth, being good and then wrong with both cases, legal information, the laws, and any other ties with these people. We all need to report what Allen did wrong, and he got away with these crimes. I said that I've been writing multiple letters to the legal authorities and have not heard anything about these letters. I said OK, calm down, and there is more about Allen. Everybody said at the same time WHAT! I said that I asked Allen for the rest of the retainer money since he lost the case and that I knew there were about 2,000 dollars that he had of my money. Allen said to me that it would take about two weeks to receive the money, and there was no indication that any money would be deducted for any reason from Allen. When I received the letter, I was thinking of a check, but it wasn't a check; instead, it was a bill for services of deductions.

Allen took about $1600.00 for the meeting about Workmen's Comp. Case visit, my phone call about the judge, and then the depositions from way back in September and October, a sum of about $1600.00. Everybody went crazy at this point; the family and Lisa said that he stole your money under the false pretense I said I agreed. But, I said, the problem is that the government officials and law officials don't want to hear anything to do with these corruption problems within their own system. So everybody asks to whom I have written these letters. I have a list starting with federal and state levels, starting with the governor of Rhode Island, the attorney general of Rhode Island, Norfolk, and Suffolk D.A. office, Butland police office, then the federal list of the justice department in Washington D.C., and here Sealand justice office, the F.B.I. office in Sealand, and then two senators of Rhode Island. The family said that this is a cover-up for the town of Butland and that all these legal authorities are ignoring the laws and citizens' rights to report crimes from top officials at the town, state, and federal levels.

CHAPTER 23
Rip-Off

    I would receive a letter from the workmen's comp. Office to report to the office for a hearing. Two days later, Attorney Allen would send an e-mail notifying me about the hearing date. On the day of the hearing, my niece Jane and I would show up for the hearing, and once again, Attorney Allen was late for our hearing with me. I asked Attorney Allen what am I supposed to expect today from the judge.? Attorney Allen said I would handle this; you will be quiet with this judge. Jane would look at me to say what? Jane said are you kidding me about this attorney? Attorney Allen would walk over to the courtroom to see Judge Jill Rip-off. Then I saw that Attorney Kerry was going into the courtroom. I got up and went to the courtroom door and called Attorney Allen; Attorney Allen came over and asked what I wanted. I said I wanted to be in the courtroom with all of you involved with my case and hear what everybody is saying. Attorney Allen said that this is a conversion for only judges and attorneys, not for you.

Jane said what the hell? This is all about you, not them. Then she said maybe they are trying to find a way to fail the case against you. I said I see things, Jane, but I can't get stressed out, then I won't be able to deal with conversations or anything at all. So I would stand in front of the door and watch them and try to listen to them. When I watched them in the courtroom, it upset all of them; then I heard the judge say, I will take care of this problem.

The judge said we were all set for the hearing to start with the attorneys, and Attorney Allen then called me into the courtroom. The judge started the hearing with introductions; I am Judge Jill Rip-off, a workmen's comp judge. Office of the Commonwealth of Rhode Island. Attorney Allen said I'm Attorney Allen Moakley, representing the plaintiff Vincent D'Angelo. Attorney Kerry said I'm Attorney Kerry Dunn representing the town of Butland. Then the judge asked me to say my name for the record Vincent D'Angelo. I said. The judge said to Attorney Allen that they would explain why we were there. Attorney Allen said that we are here because of stress-related issues related to the job with my client and the accusations of being abused by Superintendent Robert Smith with the town of Butland. The accusations are as follows mental abuse, discrimination, creating a hostile environment at the workplace, threats of losing his job, lies, and deceit from the truth of Vincent's performance, etc.; all accusations from Vince D., Angelo that Robert Smith, and the town of Butland did wrong. These have led to all types of health problems for my client. The health problems started with stomach aches which led to existing IBS problems. New problems of anxiety, fibromyalgia with widespread severe pain throughout the body, headaches severe at times, dizziness from the headaches and anxiety, confusion from the anxiety, chronic pins and needles, numbness throughout the body, the nervous system compromised from fibromyalgia, he also has some phobias. He has a future over time, of getting worse with the health problems or being more intense or new health problems from these other conditions. These health problems are attributed to stress-related difficulties because of a bully superintendent who abuses his power as a superintendent. Also, my client has told me that Robert has abused other workers in the same manner that can be called into court to testify to those allegations. The judge asked if there was anything else. Attorney Allen said no for now.

The judge asks Attorney Kerry for the town side of the complaints. Attorney Kerry would explain that all the information is a lie from the plaintiff. The plaintiff had a discriminating case that he lost. That there are no grounds for this case to go forward. Attorney Allen would say, judge, this is two different cases, and it's not irrelevant to this case here. The judge said to Attorney Kerry that there were two different cases: a civil case and this is Workmen's Comp. Case two different courtrooms and laws. The judge also said you should know this as a workmen's comp. Attorney, the judge, asked attorney Kerry if she was practicing any other law areas. Attorney Kerry said no, only Workmen's Comp. Cases.

The judge said then, well, stick to the area of law that you know. Judge Jill asked if there was any more information you would like to share with this court. Attorney Kerry would ask if she could have a minute, and the judge said yes. Attorney Kerry would recite the words of Federal Judge Dick Shawberg that Mr. D'Angelo was a lazy worker and his work was not to satisfaction with the town standards. Mr. D'Angelo was spoken to about his work habits by Robert. The town also has a letter written by his highway foreman complaining about his performance. Judge Jill said to Kerry that you are still trying to bring in another case and court results on this case; this doesn't apply or work at all for this courtroom or with me as the judge. Judge Jill said, " Are you trying to influence me as the judge and this courtroom? Kerry would say no, judge. I then started to say something about Kerry's statement to the judge, and the judge said to me that I needed to be quiet and just sit there. Jane was sitting in the back of the courtroom and heard what the judge said to me and was astonished by the judge's reply to me, trying to explain the lies of attorney Kerry and the other case of discrimination.

Judge Jill said OK, this is what we are going to do; mediation with a judge to see if an agreement can come to a better solution. The judge noticed that I wanted to say something, and then she asked what I wanted to say, Mr. D'Angelo. I said I wanted this to go to a trial with witnesses and evidence. The judge said no, first you try mediation and then maybe a hearing on this matter. As a judge, I'm explaining to you very strongly to take the mediation date, and this will relate to money and a possible settlement; if you disagree, you will have a chance to be with me as a judge. Judge Jill said you won't like the answer I give today if you disagree. Judge Jill said I will hold off on an answer to today's issues at hand till the mediation date and results. The judge released the hearing, and Allen went to talk about the hearing. Allen said that the judge wasn't happy with Kerry and brought up the other case. I asked Allen what the judge meant by telling me to take the mediation date. Allen said that she was going to deny you with today's hearing. Allen would say that we did OK for today's hearing. Allen would say that he had other clients to see today, and we parted.

Jane and I left to go to the car; Jane asked how I felt; I said I had terrible pain throughout my body. Jane asks if I can drive, I'll try to drive home, but my anxiety is starting to build up, pushing the pain throughout my body. I told Jane to watch my driving, and if I needed to pull over, I would. We would make it home, and Jane said the judge was an asshole with the whole case and then pushed you to mediation and dragged more time with this case. I said I knew. I forgot to say that it's been about five years with the judge. About two weeks later, I would receive two letters from the Workmen's Comp. Office, the first letter said three months you would have the mediation date, and the second letter said that workmen's comp. case judge Jill denied my complaints that I was in front of her that day. The judge lied about waiting for the mediation date for her decision. And on the hearing date and whether we would proceed with the case or deny the case. The judge's decision was made before we started the hearing that day, especially when the judge said to take the mediation date and force me to do that.

I called up Jane and asked her if the judge said she would wait for the end of the mediation date to decide when we saw the case judge. Jane said yes; I said the judge decided to deny for that day; I said the judge decided on the hearing even before starting; Jane asked what that meant; I said we needed to appeal the case and her decision to deny. Next, I would call Allen and ask him if he received any paperwork from w/c (workmen's comp.) Allen said no; why? I said I did, and the judge denied the case; Allen said we would appeal the decision. Allen also said that we have the mediation date, and hopefully, we will settle. I said OK to Allen, and we said goodbye. Three months later, we went back to Sealand, where it cost me another $40.00 to park every time with no income. Once again, Allen was late, and I would have my mother and daughter with me. When Allen did show up, I asked him what would happen today.

Allen said that we would see the mediation judge and try to resolve this settlement today. I was on edge with all the concerns with today's procedures with mediation. I had never been involved with anything kind of a mediation situation in my life, so I didn't know what to expect from the procedures. Judge John Mack would call for the case and handle the mediation today. Judge John would separate the two sides of the case into two separate rooms. Then the judge would go back and forth between rooms with a settlement number each time. I asked Judge John why are you separating us; I thought we would be in the same room. Judge John said no, we separate because the town side will be on the phone talking to their attorney, and you can speak to your attorney without any pressure. We started at about 9.30 am, and this would take about 3 hours to finish a settlement. During the 3 hours, the judge stared at Allen and me asking us what would be the starting number.

I said to the judge that my health problems are a lifetime of problems, the information that I have read about my health problems is the issue over time, so I'm going to start at $500,000,00. Judge John said that is not a factor in this settlement, but I will tell the other attorney the amount. Allen would say that you will not get that number. You need to come down with your numbers. I said to Allen you are kidding me? Doesn't any of my health problems come into play with this settlement? Allen would say no; I said then why are we here losing time over nothing if you aren't going to take in the health problems? Then how do you base anything on a value level? Allen said that this case is a nuisance case at this point. I said that you were the one who pushed for Workmen's Comp. Case, not me. At that moment, the judge returned with no for that amount of money, but the judge said I have a counteroffer of $ 20,000.00 I said you are kidding me; this is just a waste of my time. I knew that you all are just prolonging and making it more difficult so that I settle for a lot less of a settlement, and then to say that my health doesn't matter at this point is bull shit. The judge would say calm down, we will try to get you a comfortable settlement, so I'm assuming that you don't like $20,000.00. I said no, I don't, I said $100,000.00 to the judge, and he said that sounds more reasonable of a number. The judge left the room to talk to the town attorney, and I started to talk to Allen about the procedures of this mediation sucks. I told Allen how we knew what was happening in the other room. The judge is sitting down and having a regular conversation with us, and is he doing the same over there in the other room and wasting time? Allen said I don't know, but if he talks with us, I can assume the same is happening in the other room.

Judge John would return with an offer of $35,000.00. I said that this wasn't right. There was something wrong with these offers and procedures. I said that I had a federal judge deny me my day in court, and my case was a loss, and now I'm going through this problem over a false settlement with all of my health problems for the rest of my life with only $35,000.00. Judge John said how did that happen? Allen said that we were waiting for a court date, and the federal judge only allowed the depositions and made a decision from the depositions. Judge John said, I never heard of that issue with dismissing a case in such a way. Allen said I hope we come to an answer today because I start my vacation and will be gone for two weeks. Judge John said Well do you accept this offer? I said no, I want $50,000.00, or we go back to the case judge. Judge John would go back to the town attorney and tell her the amount; she would call the town and tell them the amount. The town would agree with the amount of $50,000.00, and Judge John would return to Allen and me and say that we have an agreement with the town for $50,000.00. After Judge John said, we had an agreement.

Kerry would walk by the door and said I have to go to my next appointment. Allen would say the same thing, but he was going on vacation, and Judge John was about to leave. I said where is Kerry going? We need to sign papers with the agreement. The judge started to speak but was interrupted by Allen, and Allen said when I get back from my vacation, we will get the papers signed then, and this will be all over for you. I said I hope so, Allen, because every time I have to explain these cases and health problems, my body goes through anxiety and pain from fibromyalgia, and that's not good for my health. It's like I'm reliving my problems repeatedly from the start. Allen said that it's all over when I get back, Vince. Allen would confirm the answer of a settlement to my mother and daughter for $50,000.00.

We would all leave the Workmen's Comp. I would explain what happened to my mother and daughter in the room on the ride home. I started explaining how they separated us and how I asked for the first amount of $500,000.00, which was denied, and then the second amount of $100,000.00 was denied; on the third, I asked for $50,000.00 the town agreed with this settlement. I said that the judge was sitting with us and having a regular conversation like he wasn't there to do his mediation job. I would have liked to know what was going on with the town attorney and Judge John. Meanwhile, Allen and I got into issues with our conversation while waiting for the judge to return. My mother and daughter said it was all over when Allen returned from his vacation. I said that another thing with Allen was the vacation, Kerry ran out after we agreed, and the judge also left in a hurry. I asked about signing the document's paperwork, and Allen said when I got back. I told Allen they could back out of this agreement; Allen said it was all over when I got back. My mother and daughter said don't worry; it's over in two weeks. I said we would see in two weeks when the check was in my hands.

Two weeks later, I called up Allen and asked if he had the papers to sign for the town's settlement. Allen said I have bad news for you, the town and attorney deny the agreement. I said what? Are you kidding me? Allen? Allen said no. Allen said that we would have to appeal the judge's decision, and now we have to go to court to argue the case. I said Allen, we have the mediation judge who can vouch that we had an agreement with the case judge. This would show how the town and attorney are lying about the whole case, and then it might offer some light on the other case as well. Allen said no, and the other case was over. I said no, Allen, if new information came up, they would have to reopen the discrimination case.

Allen said that you're mistaken with your information, and I'll get in touch with you when I get a date for the case. When I got off the phone with Allen, I explained to my mother that the town denied the settlement. Then I said that this was a planned situation and for show-and-tell games. My mother agreed that they are playing games with me and the case.

Dark Justice White Collar Crimes

CHAPTER 24
Meeting a Friend

In the summer of 2018, my family and I were invited to a family memorial for my Uncle Brian who passed away. At this memorial, I would bump into friends from work and friends of my family who live in Butland. My aunt Jerry was the wife of my uncle Brian and their children. The children were Karen, Earl, Alice, Albert, and Willy Centola. My cousins lived in Butland, RI., and my cousins were very well known, just like me being well known throughout Butland, RI., and many other towns in the area. I lived in Butland at one time, worked my jobs and business, and worked for companies in Butland; I also used to hang out and play in Butland growing up. I was the younger cousin and used to tag along with my older cousins, meet their friends, and hang out having fun in the old days of my youth. When I got older, I rented an apartment in Butland behind the old Roxie's store and had a job with a cabinet company building countertops for cabinets. When I got older with my business, I would build all types of carpentry jobs that came my way. I was all so a member of the Sons of Italy. I had many friends with whom I used to work and hang out within the town of Butland. In those days, times were good, making money and good friends and living in my apartment.

My family and I would go to the memorial; I would bump into many friends from the ZYX office and other friends from Butland. I would see friends from the ZYX office there, Richie, Moe, Scott, highway foremen, and Ryan, my other friends from Butland were Stevie, Phil, Bruce, and Mike. My cousins' friends also knew all about Butland officials' problems. When we all saw each other, we all smiled and greeted each other and started to talk about the old days. Some of the guys would ask how is your business doing. Are you still plowing for Butland? I said I was not working for myself anymore, and I did have a job with the ZYX office in Butland, but I lost the job because of Robert Smith. Then they would start asking me about what happened with the ZYX job. I said that Robert started harassing, discriminating, bullying me, and threatening my job. All my friends said I heard bad stories about Robert; they all said you aren't the first one getting screwed by Robert. Robert looks for people he can control by holding situations over their heads with threats and creating problems, especially when they don't cooperate with Robert's rules outside of the town rules. I said that happened to me because he wanted me to be a stoolie against the men at work. Robert figured I was a new employee to push around, but I wasn't that kind of a person to rat on my friends or workers from the same job. I learned a long time ago that workers and bosses have different intentions about work conditions. You need to trust your fellow workers because someday that worker may save your life, unlike bosses who don't work with the workers and just sit in an office barking orders.

When I was working with the men from the ZYX office, each of them (60 men working there) would explain that you need to worry about Robert and how he could hurt you or your job. The residents of Butland would stop me as I was plowing and complaining about Robert; it's amazing that nobody got hurt or had some type of investigation against Robert or the town hall. Robert would create all kinds of problems for the workers and residents. One of the issues is that Robert would start a problem and then intentionally set workers against each other well he did nothing to stop the problems or issues. Another problem is that Robert would use workers against other workers personally. All my friends said that Robert was notorious for the head games he played with the workers. After all of the conversations with my friend, Scott would finally say the most damaging information about Robert. First, Scott would explain Robert's suspension and how long J. B. would take over the job as acting superintendent, about two years. Then Scott said that Robert had control over the association union within the ZYX office. This wasn't a traditional Union or a regular Union. Traditional Union would have their office separate from the ZYX office or Robert. Robert controlled the association union officials and five members' offices; these men were also the same workers that Robert controlled within the ZYX office. Scott would bust open with all the information about the ZYX office and the leaders of the ZYX office and town hall leaders that were corrupt. Scott explained all the dirty deeds from the office of the ZYX office, just as he did when I was working there back in 2014 at the ZYX office. Scott said that Robert was pushed into retirement in 2015 because of his dirty deeds and the lawsuits from Vince. And Robert wasn't a threat to the workers anymore. Now the workers are talking about all the problems from Robert, including me, from 2014.

Scott would say in front of the guys (8 friends) that all the workers were trying to give you Vince the information about all the problems within the ZYX office because we knew that Robert would dismiss you from your job. The reason was that Robert would have other plans for you, Vince, and many other new workers or new employees that would come in over time, and Robert would discriminate against the worker in some way. Scott said that Robert couldn't just keep saying that the workers are just not fitting in or insufficient workers; people would catch on with the same complaints. Robert would be creative in dismissing workers without showing too much information or knowledge on how he did things wrong against the worker. He would cover up situations till you brought a lawsuit against him and the town. The other side of the problem was the town hall would also protect Robert most of the time till he was suspended and other problems from Robert that he created. When he let you go from your job, this would raise some eyebrows within the town hall, and Robert would be forced to retire from his office and job. Scott would say that Robert was to retire in 2017 but instead retired in 2015, about a year after you left. This decision came down from the town hall office, with the two lawsuits you set against the town and Robert pushing the selectmen and other officials where they had enough of Robert's creating problems for the town. Scott said that before you came into the job, Robert and two other ZYX office workers got a very high raise, and Robert got like an 80% raise to him. Scott said that you were the fall guy with Robert, and Robert was the fall guy after Robert did what he did to you with the town hall officials.

    Scott would say, Vince, I'm sorry for what happened to you with your job and the issue that Robert made me write that letter about you and your work habits and lied in with this letter. Robert had the control to terminate men on the job or make their job very difficult working here at the ZYX office. Scott said we all have families; I said so, I also have a family too. I would also lose my health for a lifetime, with pain every day and the possibility of being in a wheelchair, with a lot more than the doctors don't know about my health or my future. Meanwhile, our friends heard all the information that Scott said. Scott would say that I'm not finished with all the information from the town. I said to Scott that I'm having a hard time taking in all of this information, I have many health problems, and I would like to record your information to present this to law enforcement and proper authorities. I also want you and the other guys to verify the stories you heard from Scott. The guys would say that many people knew that Robert would hurt you and your job and many other people over time, past and present. The town also protects Robert by retiring him so that he would preserve his pension as well. I said that I knew that you didn't have the information about me being ill or hurt by these actions from Robert. But now you know of my health problems, and you don't want to help me set the record straight? Scott said you don't understand our families and the problems the town can cause; I said that's why we stand together and fight these problems of conspiracy level with the town and Robert. Then I had my conspiracy fight with the doctors, attorneys, and the judges, along with all the letters I wrote to ask for help and an investigation of these cases. I said you all would show the town, state, and country that they are not untouchable; they are just as responsible for their actions of criminal offenses as white-collar crimes. I also said to my friends that Robert wanted me to be a rat to you guys, and I chose not to do that or be a stoolie. If the town officials have that much power, then what do the state and country have for control? I said that this might explain why I haven't heard anything from my letters to all of the authorities I wrote to explain the problems.

The memorial function for my uncle would come to an end for the night. I would have more knowledge of what happened with Robert and the town with me being involved with a cover-up and a conspiracy from them. The next day I would see if my family could come over, and I would explain all the information that I found out about Butland at the function. My mother said that we all would have dinner together and talk about the information that we heard from our friends. Everybody came for dinner, and I started to explain what my friends said as we were eating dinner. I remind my family of my travels over my time about my living, working, customers, friends, family, and members of Sons of Italy in Butland. I said that I have been throughout Butland all my life, plus other towns. Then because of this memorial function for Uncle Arthur, my friends from the ZYX office realized and noticed that they allowed Robert and the town hall to hurt and destroy a man's life. The threat to their jobs and families weighs more than just one man at a time. But now they are seeing and hearing from me; now they realize that they made a mistake allowing Robert and town hall to do all this damage to other people from the past and me. Then Scott said a lot of information about Robert and town hall and all the wrong they all do in Butland. Then Scott said that Robert made him write the letter about me being a bad worker for the town. Scott also said that Robert made him lie about the letter's contents. Scott then explains how the town protected Robert and protected his pension because of my lawsuits against them. If the pension board found out that Robert had criminal influence over his job, he would lose his pension. I was set up for failure with the town because of Robert and his corrupt ways.

The entire family started to talk with frustration, and the thoughts that they were saying could cause significant legal problems for us all. I said that I understood the feeling, but we can't act this way. It is illegal. I said that there are other ways of handling problems of illegal situations from Robert and the town situation. The town controls the crimes (white-collar crime leaders) and Robert (blue-collar crimes and muscle), so we need to write the letters repeatedly till someone answers these letters. Joseph asked if my friends would come forward with this information; I said no, the threat is too serious with the town and Robert, plus they live in the town that would have consequences. I even asked if I could record them and their accurate information, and they said no. I said that I would find a way of handling these problems on a legal level, unlike a criminal way like the town and Robert. I said that paperwork and a paper trail are the worst things in the world for criminals and can be used against the town and Robert. I said the main problem is getting the law officials to read the letters and listen to the public and my complaints about these problems. I said that the unknown rules of the government are to put the people against each other at all times, so we can try to reverse that situation on the law and government. I said that once we prove that the beginning of the story is a big lie, then everything after that is a giant conspiracy that would include the attorneys, doctors, judges, and anyone I wrote letters to; this would be like a domino effect with law and government and the whole story.

CHAPTER 25
Government, Laws & the C.D.C.

When God created heaven and earth, God created a world within seven days. God had his own rules and laws to follow when he made the earth (Genesis; King James Bible). Then God created man and woman on the earth with a set of rules and laws from God. As time passed, God would set forth a new set of laws for the world to obey and follow. They would be called the Ten Commandments.

God made the first laws of our world; they were called the Ten Commandments.

1. You shall have no other gods before me. 2. You shall make no idols. 3. You shall not take the name of the Lord your God in vain. 4. Keep the sabbath day holy. 5. Honor your father and your mother. 6. You shall not

murder. 7. You shall not commit adultery. 8. You shall not steal. 9. You shall not bear false witness against your neighbor. 10. You shall not covet.

From the beginning of time, law and order were always necessary for the universe, our worlds, planets, and the people of the land. As society started to grow and new nations were born, the world grew more prominent. The laws of the land will grow in time, as our civilization will grow in time. There would increase in new laws and order throughout the ages. The laws and order will be a challenge over time and generations. The laws of God were made for equality between men and women and throughout the land over a long time of man's existence. Instead, God's laws and humanity's laws would be broken repeatedly over the ages. Men would break the laws and order in so many new ways that the laws would have to change just as fast to keep up with the criminals over the ages.

The world will adapt to multiple new & old laws and order; in present times. Before technology, crimes started with spears, knives, swords, bows, and arrows, and over time would only get more devious weapons and strategic ways our government and laws have put people against each other in time. The greed of having an empire like the Egyptians, Romans, and then the rest of Europe would follow along with many other nations of people that would have their time as an empire. Slavery would come from conquering other nations and countries, with wars from that time more significant than anyone could imagine then or in today's world. The reason was the brutal bloodshed from these weapons of past and present. When gunpowder was invented, this was the start of new technology, and shortly after that was the steam engine invention. By the 1900s, combustible engines were being invented with many other inventions like electricity and gas for combustible engines. From the 1900s forward, technology increased unbelievably, and so did the crimes and criminals. The immigrants that came to America would also bring their criminal ways with them, and the politicians and leaders would be the greedy ones with their wealth and controlling powers.

Today's world is run by computers and is more dangerous than any weapon manufactured in the past. Today's computers control our worst weapons of destruction to the planet Earth and to everything you can think of phones, cars, appliances, etc. The computers also acted as a paper trail that would never be erased, unlike actual paper that would get destroyed somehow. It's a permanent record that will follow you and your family well beyond after you die, just like the history of the world in our books. The lies that people can say or do in any way can and will be typed into the computers for a permanent record. Once typed into the computer, no one can dispute these lies or just a simple erase, and once the information is done, the damages are done as well. The criminal's leaders or the criminal life know how these things would work, so they would do something in the shadows without any public knowledge or with honest people who would uphold this country's laws. The United States of America is being run by our government officials and leaders who have been criminals since discovering these continents, America's. The government also allows criminal action from outside forces that have always hurt the world's people as we know it to be. Hence, the start of white-collar crimes; would start with power, greed, stealing the land wealth, and the lies from our government of American dreams that did a lot of damage to our people of the past and present.

The laws are no different from our government which is the people that make the laws. The actual or intentional mistakes conducted from the start of any investigation are despicable. They can or have broken the laws of the citizens' rights and the rights of laws in this country. In my cases, I ask for an investigation from all of the proper authorities of law, government, media, and friends who said their jobs would be on the line to be fired; no man, woman, or child should ever be afraid of reporting any crimes of criminals. I also try to report complaints to the town police and file reports with the governor, attorney general office, and senators of Rhode Island with no results. I have also reported to my doctors and challenged the doctors with the C.D.C. office information with no results. The information from the computer that I have spent a lot of time looking up these laws and medical information. And overall knowledge of how I would follow the laws myself and do the right thing for me and my cases with bad results. Then, I was told not to follow the computer's information about legal information or medical information from the attorneys and doctors. It was amusing when I was told not to follow the laws or medical information that comes from the legal books of law and the C.D.C. website and much more info from the computer. Computers were invented for the facts of educational reasons and many other reasons, but when used to prove your point on a subject, you are told not to follow the computer against them. In today's world, computers are used by all top officials like the justice department, senators, governors, attorney general, attorneys, judges, doctors, and police departments. You can have a history lesson from a computer of all the crimes and other information that the leaders and officials have done over time and throughout our history table. When a man stands alone with complaints about the law and medical systems, people should get involved because one day, this can be you with a losing battle with officials, laws, doctors, and medical information reasons. Never leave a person behind for any reason.

    Remember our constitution of America, the true words that were said, and the true thoughts behind these words of our constitution. Today, the Constitution has no meaning to our country, government leaders, or even the general public anymore in today's world. It's just a piece of parchment paper with no meaning to our government or the people. Our government uses the constitution for convenience, just like the laws; we have a government that can't even get along in the office or the capital. Our government expects the citizens to get along with each other. Our U.S. Government teaches the country and the world; that if they can't follow the laws they made for the ordinary good citizens, then why would they expect the country or world to follow the laws? Remember that shit rolls downhill from our president to the homeless people on our streets. Our government isn't doing its job correctly in any way, shape, or form, including in all official offices. We, the people of America, should take back our government and fire all existing governments. Then the people should hire a new government that will uphold the laws of this country and then put a ceiling on their pay, limit terms of office, and conditions of being held responsible for all actions well in office even after they leave their office. Then, the taxes can be used for better conditions and reasons and cut back the taxes. Overall, we, the people, are just slaves in paying the taxes to our U.S. Government, as our government does wrong for Americans and worldwide, especially when the government breaks the laws. Remember that only a few things don't discriminate in life; one is death; it doesn't matter the color, religion, rich or poor, health or sickness, or any other thing in our world. The other one for Americans is the taxman, or our U.S. Government doesn't discriminate when collecting taxes; either you pay or jail time for those who violate the tax laws.

When anybody reports any criminal complaint to the proper authorities of law and government officials, it should be taken seriously and not pushed off or ignored. Unfortunately, this isn't true with my cases or the people in charge of law and order. The professionals involved with my cases, doctors attorneys, and judges never took the time to hear me complain. Even professional people like doctors have a significant say with all medical information needed for the attorneys and judges for accurate results of law and order. Remember, the little people make up the population that needs help from all the intruders of criminal offenses, including white-collar crimes, that control our country and world. There are a lot of white-collar crimes that are not even reported because they don't even receive the acknowledgment that they deserve for the reason of rich and powerful people behind the white-collar crimes. This is one of the reasons it's against the law to record any crime with a video or audio recorder. This is your only proof of catching white-collar crimes and criminals. Especially when it has to do with high officials or rich people taking advantage of people; it's ok for the law to listen in on conversations of the mafia, drug dealers, and all other crimes; otherwise, forget about it; it isn't happening for a regular person to record officials or government involved with crimes. Real crimes start in an office where the law and government officials commit these white-collar crimes. This is how the controversy starts with our government and leaders and secret societies that control our world. The laws don't fit the problems of today's world. It only includes the rich and powerful to commit these white-collar crimes and have their ways. Our government and laws are to set an excellent example of people's rights with laws and order. Our country is a product of history that was wrong from the beginning, with the laws of the land and people's rights being violated time and time again. Then you wonder why we have more blue-collar crimes committed every day against each other for survival or personal gain.

The reality of our government, politicians, laws, secret societies, law enforcement on all levels, banks, corporations, and other leaders worldwide are the problems of our world and how criminals get away with these white-collar crimes. Politicians are the planners of crimes in our world. And they allow blue-collar crimes to come about in our world. The teachers need muscle to enforce the dirty deeds and tactics of forcing regular people to do as the leaders want in their favor. Examples are two presidents John F. Kennedy and Abraham Lincoln were murdered by our government leaders. The government hired assassins to carry out blue-collar crimes of murder. There are so many criminal elements right in front of your own eyes, and you don't even think about or act in any way, shape, or form. As the regular people, we are also to blame for the murders of two presidents; we, the people, have the power to fire the leaders and put them behind bars in prisons for the crimes of killing two presidents.

In 2016 President Trump was our president, and he treated his presidency as a corporation and business, not as a personal gain like the other politicians. As a result, the country started to prosper with the economy and finances; our borders are safer with no drugs crossing the borders and the immigrants illegally crossing the borders. President Trump's battles between Capitol Hill and other government officials attacking every step he made were despicable for government leaders. The weird issue is that our government treats President Trump and citizens as the children of this country, and government officials are the mothers and fathers of our country. But when the proper father (President Trump) came into the office, with the secondary mothers and fathers had so many complaints that they had no standing when the father (President Trump) spoke. When the end of every day comes, our wonderful government is carrying on with secrets from other leaders, breaking the laws that the government invented, and outright lying to our people and country. When will the citizens of true Americans take a stand against our government? When are the citizens of America going to say that's enough with our government; and fire all these people from their office? Remember the history of the past empires falling because of the uprise of the people getting tired of the lies and betrayal of their government. Will history repeat in our present time? Our President Joe Biden is the new puppet on the strings of our government. President Biden has his falls, with the public and citizens, and even with different government branches. There should be an age cut-off for any government office and not have 70-year-old people in the office. In all the years that have passed, we never had a good president to run our country that everybody agreed with, and we never will.

CHAPTER 26
Primary Doctor & the C.D.C.

I would take the time to try to explain to Dr. Lori Iceburg the seriousness of my cases and my medical records and information for judges and courts. I had an appointment coming up with Dr. Lori. This time I would bring the information from the C.D.C. website as I did with Dr. Peter. Meanwhile, my family and I didn't understand why my doctors weren't cooperating with the cases or my attorney. My family believes that the doctors are not doing their job right or professionally. Maybe there is an alternative reason why the doctors weren't cooperating with my attorney or me. My family and I started thinking about a bribe from the town to the doctors or something along those lines. If there were any type of bribe from the town, this would be a significant problem for me, my two cases, attorneys, judges, courts, and justice of our laws. This would explain why the doctors weren't cooperating or why the doctors were just incompetent.

I would think about why a doctor or doctors wouldn't back up a patient with health reasons of mental disability or physical disability. I would look over the medical records that I have, and there was a lot of information about my illnesses. However, I noticed that no doctors had (PTSD) post-traumatic stress disorder in my medical records or illnesses. The doctors had all of the other symptoms and conditions related to PTSD, plus other health conditions outside of PTSD problems. PTSD problems are a mental disability that includes symptoms of intrusive memories, avoidance, negative changes in thinking and mood, changes in physical and emotional reactions, anxiety, and depression. All of my health problems are related to stress issues, and problems include IBS, fibromyalgia, tension headaches, and nervous system problems. Then you have the secondary problems of pain in the joints and muscles with other secondary problems. So when I looked up the C.D.C. information, I found this with PTSD, another stress-related problem that wasn't in my medical records or the doctors were keeping that out of my records.

INTRUSIVE MEMORIES:

Recurrent, unwanted distressing memories of the traumatic event.

Examples: boss bullying, harassment on the job, racial discrimination on the job, verbal abuse.

Reliving the traumatic event as if it were happening again (flashbacks).

Example: explaining the incidents to doctors, attorneys, therapy counsels, and judges. With nobody believing the incidents.

Upsetting dreams or nightmares about the traumatic event.

Severe emotional distress or physical reactions to something that reminds you of the traumatic event.

Example: my job with the town and the treatment from a boss.

AVOIDANCE:

Trying to avoid thinking or talking about the traumatic event.

Example: locked in a room sleeping all the time.

Avoid places, activities, or people that remind you of the traumatic event.

Example: Claims of pain, dizziness, and headaches from fibromyalgia.

NEGATIVE CHANGES IN THINKING AND MOOD:

Negative thoughts about yourself, other people, or the world.

Hopelessness about the future.

Memory problems include not remembering important aspects of the traumatic event.

Difficulty maintaining close relationships.

Feeling detached from family and friends.

Lack of interest in activities you once enjoyed.

Difficulty experiencing positive emotions.

Feeling emotionally numb.

CHANGES IN PHYSICAL AND EMOTIONAL REACTIONS:

Being easily startled or frightened.

Always being on guard for danger.

Self-destructive behavior, such as drinking too much or driving too fast.

Trouble sleeping.

Trouble concentrating.

Irritability, angry outbursts, or aggressive behavior.

Overwhelming guilt or shame.

This is one of many pieces of information that I look for and research with medical, legal, and laws. Then to read my medical records and found nothing about PTSD in my medical records. I couldn't believe that my doctors, psychiatrist, and therapy counselor did not see these symptoms of PTSD with all of the other stress-related problems. But on the other hand, these doctors weren't writing any medical information for attorney Allen to admit the facts of my medical records either. The scary part is that these professional doctors had eight years of schooling; before becoming a doctor, and they didn't see any of the symptoms of PTSD problems. I know I don't hold the title of a doctor or an attorney, but I'm smarter than my doctors, attorneys, judges, and all involved with my cases. All I had to do was look up all the information online with the internet and websites, and they wasted eight years of studying when I took hours to research my information. I would also pass in medical papers from independent doctors, and my doctors said that I made up these papers and didn't believe the medical documents that were given to the judges on these cases. This would also lead to the fact that the medical records were being ignored simultaneously. When I saw how the medical records were being ignored, that also meant that all information that the attorneys and judges had were false medical records. These would lead to false legal documents and judgments, like a set of dominos falling right after another.

The day came for my doctor's visit with Dr. Iceberg. I would enter the examining room, and the nurse would do the vital signs and ask about my medicine; then, she would say that the doctor would be in soon. The doctor came in, and we greeted each other; Dr. Lori asked how is your health doing. I said to Dr. Lori that my pains are getting worse every year, the weather controls my pains, I'm getting more headaches, my feet, hands, and joints are killing me, my muscles are starting to hurt, and chest pains and I have a new problem with my spine hurting throughout the day and night. All of the pains keep me up, or the pains will wake me up throughout the night. I also have dreams that make no sense. I told you about the spots on my feet, the stabbing pain throughout my body, and my inching. While explaining my condition, Dr. Lori typed the information into her computer. Dr. Lori asked if I was taking my medicine; I said yes when I needed to. Why don't you take medicine the way I prescribe it to you? I said I'm sensitive to the medicine, and I don't know why. I explain the pain medicine knocks me out, and the muscle relaxer does the same for two days; if I take medicine the way you prescribe, I'll never see the world again because I'll sleep my life away. I asked Dr. Lori if she had received the x-rays from Dr. Peter Orlando, and she said no. I told you to look up the X-rays because they can explain some of my pain. Dr. Lori said to explain to me what Dr. Peter said to you. I have bone spurs and bone loss in my neck, middle of the back bulging disc, and my lower back has a bulging disc along with arthritis; then my hips have some bone shaving that looks like a diamond effect, another word my hip sockets aren't round they have sides that were worn down.

Dr. Lori said that I couldn't find the X-rays. I told Dr. Lori that I was getting worse and not working, so how was my body going through these new problems? Is it because of fibromyalgia? Then I ask what are you going to do for me? Dr. Lori said I don't have an answer for you; I believe you are faking your injuries, and you should go back to work. Inside my mind, that was the switch that set me off. I said Well, doctor, you are 100% wrong; let's start with x-rays that you don't want to believe, and then Dr. Peter you don't want to believe, then the independent doctors from the town, court, and my independent doctor that you don't believe, why, what is your problem?

Dr. Lori was quiet; then, I began to explain the work of researching the internet for medical answers. Dr. Lori interrupted me and said that the C.D.C. has no say in my office. I explained that the C.D.C. has all the rights in your office because they are a government-run and top medical officials' office. I also found this information about stress-related problems related to me and my health. Why haven't you diagnosed me with PTSD, especially the psychiatrist and therapy counselor? Once again, Dr. Lori was quiet; I said that the records I had read had all the signs of mental stress, and you don't have PTSD in my records. I said that you have medical doctors and reports with X-rays, ignoring the facts. I said you are violating my rights, personal and health, and our country's laws. You are withholding medical information from the courts, which is punishable under federal and state laws. The problem could affect all of the doctors involved in my two cases. You know how this would affect a person/patient with mental stress to prove this to a judge or court. It's very hard and difficult to prove anything in a courtroom without the proper documents from a doctor or doctors.

I said to Dr. Lori that you are the doctors who know mental health problems, and you are not admitting the facts into my records and my cases of stress-related problems. I explain that I see TV commercials with more compassion for people with health problems, especially mental stress or mental health problems. We have hotlines for all types of health issues or problems to try and help the people, and here you are in person with me, and you can even see the facts from your records to other doctors or from your patient. That is me as your patient and a person. It's like you disregard my explanation of how things happen to me and the outcome of my health. It's a well-known fact that people with their jobs can get stressed out from the job alone, then add the facts of a boss coming at you with bullying, harassing, discriminating, and just being rotten to people. And the same boss goes around bragging about how he gives a hard time to people intentionally on the job. Now I have doctors, attorneys, judges, and all the people I have written to complain to about my problems of criminal actions and still got no results for the better. Don't you think this will take a toll on a regular person? Now add in the fact of a person with multiple stress disorders. Dr. Lori said Well, if you don't like my services, then find another doctor. I asked why it wasn't already in my records (PTSD), and nobody took this seriously. A new doctor or attorney will only give the town attorney the power to say I was shopping around for a doctor or attorney, which would only make me look bad in front of the judge. So, no, I can't do this with you or my attorney or other doctors, plus nobody wants to pick up the shit you caused or anybody else's shit. Nobody wants to go through your records and sort out the facts after messing up everything. I said you couldn't even get social security insurance, right? I said remember that when this is over with my cases, I will have an investigation about the whole problem. The medical, legal, and court records will show the proof, along with the witnesses of how professional people take advantage of a person with mental stress, health problems, and legal problems.

Dark Justice White Collar Crimes

CHAPTER 27
Attorney Allen

Attorney Allen and workmen's comp. office would send a notice of going to the Sealand office for a hearing. I would set up a meeting with Attorney Allen so that we can talk about the Workmen's Comp. Case. Attorney Allen said through an e-mail to come in on Monday at 10.00 am, and he added that the town gave another offer. Monday came, and I was there with my mother, and we greeted Attorney Allen at his office. I started asking about the mediation judge and settlement offer; attorney Allen said that's over. I said doesn't the case judge need to be notified about this settlement offer being revoked by the town attorney and town?

Allen would say no, she doesn't need to know about this refusal from the town or town attorney. I said to Allen; I hope you are right with your answer? Attorney Allen said that Attorney Kerry called with another offer of $35,000.00. Are you interested in this offer? Allen said you would not get a better offer, and I think you should take this offer. Once again, Allen hit my key, and I was upset with his explanation; I said Allen, you have information on this case that should prove that lies and tricks are being played with us, or is this just me being played out by you? Allen would say that you are incorrigible. You think that people are against you, and they are not; it's the way the laws work. It's what you can prove in a court of law and not hearsay. I said you are right and wrong; if my attorney doesn't bring the correct facts and evidence forward to the judge, you are wrong. I agree that you need the facts and evidence for a judge to make a proper judgment Allen.

The other problem is that Judge Jill was to wait for an answer on the last court date from the mediation judge, and that's why I asked if Judge Jill was to be notified of the results. I told Allen that I have talked to other attorneys to help me and guide me with you and my cases. Allen said that's why I say you are incorrigible. You don't stop looking for problems. I said Allen; I need an attorney that is not lying to me; I need an attorney who will do his job correctly and not deceive me or cover up anything with these cases. I alone and we together know the truth about the town and their attorneys are lying about the whole problem and that I was set up with Robert and then the town trying to save their asses. Then I said that if anyone falsified any medical or legal records, this is a federal and state offense of the laws of this country, Allen. Allen said I know the laws, don't worry, Vince, I said in return, I know of too many people who say I know things and were also liars, then I had to deal with the problems myself many times. Allen, I'm not afraid of the problems or consequences. That's for the other people to worry about, not me. Then Allen tried to defuse the situation and bring up workmen's comp. Questions and answers. I said I needed to go to the bathroom; Allen said OK.

While I was in the bathroom, my mother would start explaining to Allen that my son had lost everything in his life; how do you think he's feeling right now with all lying, deceiving, hurting, and other feelings like failing? As a man. He gave up his business for the town; he gave the town about 12 years of plowing and made friends at that time; when the town hired him as an employee, he thought that all of his troubles would be gone, but that didn't happen for Vince. Instead, he picks up more significant problems that push him over the edge with mental stress problems. Now you have no cooperation from doctors, attorneys, judges, or the letters he wrote. My mother told Allen that my son needed this job to work for himself, and I know he did his best for the town. When he was plowing for the town, Robert was always complemented by his plowing and work ethic. I even remember when Vince shows up before the town employees, and Robert yells at Vince for being in too soon and before the town workers. I also remember when Vince was hired and before the new year, Vince was getting compliments from everybody at work, saying an excellent job on the windows. Then after the new year, everything started to fall apart for Vince because of one man named Robert; everybody else was happy with Vince's work. Allen would interrupt and say why are the foremen complaining about his work? My mother said to think about it; Allen, Robert is the main boss of the ZYX office. Do you think Robert may be corrupted, incompetent, or something wrong with the man? My son came home and explained how you nailed the two bosses at the depositions and with you saying that they don't have a straight answer and are lying. Allen didn't know what to say at this point to my mother. My mother then said that you and my son lost the discrimination case in federal court; why Allen? Allen didn't even have an answer for that question either. Allen looked pretty bad after my mother talked to him with guilt on his face and asked if he accepted a payoff of some kind from the town.

I would return from the bathroom, notice Allen's face, and wonder what had happened. I sat down and then asked what we to expect from this judge that treated me like shit the last time and made a judgment. She said she would wait to hear about the mediation date to give us a judgment; she denied me on the hearing day. Allen said I don't know what to say to you, Vince. Allen said that I had news about the offer from the town. You asked for a meeting about the case; I said yes, I did, but you're the attorney, and you must have a plan to present this case to the judge. Since we will file an appeal and go to court, do we need witnesses for this court time? Allen said yes, we would need witnesses; Allen asked me who I wanted to be a witness. I looked at him funny and said what do you mean, Allen? You are to think of the people you need to help explain and prove the conditions of my job problems, and then my family members to explain the home condition, and then the doctors to explain the health conditions. Why am I telling you about your job and how to prove this case when you should be telling my mother and me instead? You, as the attorney, should be putting us at ease with these problems of these cases. Then you don't understand why I'm so upset with you and why I may question you and your actions. Once again, Allen would just push off the questions and say give me a list of people you want as witnesses. I said I'll give it to you now; Allen said, no, I have another client coming. Allen said to send me an e-mail with the list of witnesses, and I'll see you in Sealand on that date. I said, OK, Allen and I left Allen's office upset, and my mother said I'll speak to you in the car.

My mother and I got in the car, and we started to talk about what was said to Allen. I asked what happened when I went to the bathroom, mother? Before I explained that Allen is a piece of shit and sucks as an attorney, my mother said. My mother said she was so upset with his conversation that you asked the right question, and Allen was not answering or just avoiding the questions. My mother said that you need to find another attorney to handle this part of the case; I believe that Allen will leave you high and dry when you need him the most. I told my mother he had already done that to me with the discrimination case, and we lost. I had no time to find an attorney to help with the appeal to the federal court. Sarah and I tried to write some kind of appeal within the ten days, but we lost that too. I asked my mother what happened with Allen; my mother said I explain how bad you are at home fighting doctors, attorneys, lies from the town, judges, and the letters you wrote to people. Then my mother added that's why you saw his face the way you did; he didn't expect me to speak up about the whole problem to him. My mother said you would sue him in court after this is over and all the rest. About a week later, just before court day, I received a bill again from Allen charging me for a visit to his office last week. I showed my mother and my family, and they all said that he was overcharging and stealing your retainer money. I said when it comes to Workmen's Comp. Case there is no charge till Allen wins the case.

The day of Workmen's Comp. Office. I would show up with my niece Jane and my mother. As usual, Attorney Allen would be late; Allen would check in with the desk, acknowledging that he and his client were here for the hearing that day. I was still upset with Allen because of the bill he sent and many other reasons for the disaster between Allen and me. Allen asked how we were doing today; I and my family and I said OK. I asked him if he had heard anything from the town attorney Kerry; Allen said no. I asked him if he knew what would happen today, and Allen said no. When I heard his answers, inside of me, I wanted to kick the shit out of him so bad, but I didn't need to go to jail for a stupid problem I caused. Especially where money and a lawsuit were involved, I just wanted this case to end as soon as possible. Unfortunately, this case would carry on for another two years, with many crimes being committed by both attorneys and four judges altogether at Workmen's Comp. Office.

Judge Jill would call in the two attorneys and have their little talk, and they stopped me from being in the room with them. My mother and Jane called me over and said that's why our law system is so corrupted; this is about you, and you can't hear what they are saying about you or the case. For all we know, they are making a deal to intentionally fail the case before you have a chance of justice. I said what nobody sees or hears is OK, but when somebody makes a verbal threat, it's against the law; the sad part is that people just don't say things wrong for no reason; it is always for a reason when they make verbal threats or physical actions. Just like me saying, white-collar crimes are in motion with both of my cases, and all the professional people are at fault for white-collar crimes. There is a verbal and physical threat here, but it is legal and within the laws of this country. But when you make these accusations about professional people, they suddenly mark you as a threat and finish you in some horrible way. For example, two presidents and many other people in the world, the wrong people, have succeeded many times. I said that this world and people had been screwed over so many times and in so many ways, personal, business, gender, color, religion, age, and just about any way that a person can hurt you in this world of yesterday or today. The sad part is that nobody can understand the hurt and revenge that a person would feel from the hurt and loss they carry in their mind or in other ways. The worst part of our government is that the conspiracists and terrorists are one of the same. Our government divides and conquers the people of our world, and nobody is stopping them from doing as they please in destroying everything and everybody.

Judge Jill finally called for me to be in the courtroom. My family members and I went into the courtroom and sat down. Judge Jill would start by asking attorney Allen has there had been any progress with the case. Allen said no. Judge Jill asked attorney Kerry what the condition of this case was, and Kerry asked the judge to dismiss the case again. Judge

Jill said that couldn't happen; we needed a solution for this case. Allen said that we would appeal your decision, and we requested for independent evaluation by a doctor to clear up questions about Vince and his health problems. The judge asked if Kerry agreed with this request; Kerry said yes, I have a problem with this request because there is no cause for this request. Kerry said this man wasn't sick; this was just a lie to receive some money from the town. The judge asked Kerry if she was qualified to make this diagnosis as a doctor or a judge. Kerry said no, your judge. The judge asks whether there is a reason why you're telling your answer. Kerry said that I'm not at liberty to explain at this time. Kerry then said that it relates to our conversation from early on.

Then the judge said yes, you're right; ok, well, we will have to wait for the results when the time comes, and I will take action then. I would look back at my family as a question with the look in my eyes to say what was happening here. The judge said that we need to have an independent evaluation for Vince, and we go from there. Allen would explain that I was disadvantaged by the expense of the two cases at this time; we needed the state to cover the cost of the evaluation. The judge said that's fine, have Vince fill out the paperwork for this. The judge asked if there were any other matters at this time. The attorneys said no. I said yes, judge, I have something to say.

The judge got all upset with my answer. I said I like to know about your conversation before the hearing, and it sounds like some laws are being broken. From me reading into this conversation during the hearing, the judge said that has no business of yours. I said yes, it does because if you're breaking the laws and hiding the facts of what is going wrong, that is a problem for everybody involved with this case. I said that you think you can talk around me and that I'm a stupid person or mentally challenged, I'm not. From the start of the town until now, about five years later, people are just lying, as attorney Kerry said, but it's not me. I said that everybody is just ignoring mental stress on the job, especially when you have a boss implying the problem of this stress to an employee, including me. Then you all debate whether it is true without any witnesses from my job or other people. The facts are right in front of your face; ignoring them and making up your own rules to fit the case.

Meanwhile, you have all of these stress-related problems in this state about marathon bombings, black lives matter, and our government that acts like children in the office and can't agree on anything for the people. I said this is a joke about our laws; you don't want justice. You want controversy and problems and divide the people to conquer them later. One of the issues is that people with mental problems are being pushed aside or ignored; in my case, I have a man who causes my problem, and you allow him to get away with this problem. The judge asked if I was done, and I said not really but for now. The judge said we were all set for this session. I asked Allen what kind of doctor will I see. Allen said that it would be a psychiatrist. I said what about a rheumatologist doctor who can explain my fibromyalgia related to my stress problems and pain. I said to Allen that this is one of the main problems I have Allen. Allen once again just ignored me again.

CHAPTER 28

Independent Contractors

Two new doctors would see me for the independent evaluation; the first doctor was from the town, Dr. Green. The second doctor was from the courts, Dr. Weinberg. The town attorney had a schedule to get the doctor's report in on time, and the same for the court doctor with a schedule. I would hear all different stories about the opposite side of doctors lying and deceiving medical records to win their cases, for the town in my case. The time of the year was the fall time of 2019. The day came when I had the town evaluation with Dr. Green. I would take my niece Jane with me for the doctor's visit and as a witness. Unfortunately, attorney Kerry would not send Dr. Green the medical records, and other information (Robert's deposition) about the cases wasn't on time before my appointment.

Why would a doctor need deposition information for a medical evaluation? Attorney Kerry was trying to alter the effect of being late to return the medical evaluation to the court. As a result, the town evaluation would not be allowed as evidence for the town side. Attorney Kerry would argue with Senior Judge Bill Child of the workmen's comp. Office. Senior Judge Bill said the laws state that if you go past the date expiration with evidence, it is all over with that information, and I cannot allow you to break the laws. Kerry would be upset with his answer. But Kerry was also busy looking into an investigation company to follow me around and document the everyday things I did. So, this is what made things difficult with being on time for the evaluation. The same situation was discussed in the last court time under secrets talk with the judge and attorneys.

The evaluation with Dr. Green was very difficult for me because of my anxiety, which triggered my fibromyalgia pain throughout my whole body. Dr. Green explained that he didn't have the medical records and would evaluate without the information. He didn't explain that he would have other information about the cases. Dr. Green said what do you think happened at your job in your own words. I knew that he used a psychological approach to break down my guard when I heard these words. The stories that I heard were true with these types of doctors. The questions would go on with him, and I noticed he dissected my story to see if I was lying about my health and job problems. I would explain that there are witnesses to some of these actions of claim from my job. I also explained that my doctors wrote up the medical records, not me. I said I don't understand what this evaluation is about; as far as my job, that is for a court to decide, not you, and as far as medical records, you should talk to my doctors for answers or have the documents. These questions are for a judge to listen to and not an independent doctor, especially when you don't have the records. I said that my job stressed me out by one man bullying me, harassing me, and discriminating remarks on the job. The people are lying about the whole situation, including the attorneys and judges. I said that all that was involved in trying to protect the town from a lawsuit. I'm not having this happen; I will prove that the town and Robert lie about the beginning to everything after, and everybody involved lies about the cases. Dr. Green said are you sure about these accusations; I said yes. After 2.5 hours later, with senseless questions, he finally said that we were done. Two weeks later, I would have received the report from Dr. Green and the fact that attorney Kerry didn't get the report in on time with the court. Dr. Green's report was all lies about nothing that was needed in a courtroom, and in a single sentence, he said that I should go to work and that I was faking my health problems and lied about the job problem with Robert.

I would receive paperwork to see the independent doctor, Dr. Weinberg, from the w/c court. Once again, I would take my niece Jane to the appointment. We would arrive early, just like all my appointments. The doctor said just sit down, and I will be with you in a few minutes. My anxiety started, and fibromyalgia pain became the main problem. The stress of all these doctors and legal appointments; and explaining my story with the complaints are taking a toll on my life and health, which is unbelievable. Dr. Weinberg asked me to come in and sit down so we could start. Dr. Weinberg introduced himself and said that he was requested to be evaluated by the w/c court. The doctor said I need a license to prove who you are, I would show him my license, and he made a copy of the license. Then Dr. Weinberg said, I have read your records, and now I want you to explain your knowledge of your problems. Dr. Weinberg said that I'm not for any side of this case; I am here for just an evaluation on you only so you can be candid with me. Once again noticed how people tried to break your guard and use a psychological approach with questions. The problem I had was that my guard was always up; because I was deceived so many times. Starting with Robert and then up to the present time with many people over time with these cases. This would include all doctors, attorneys, judges, and state and federal agencies that I have complained to, and nobody was concerned with my complaints about the laws or justice that were being broken.

I would explain the legal problems, health problems, and complaints to Dr. Weinberg. I would also take a chance to try to trust someone, which was Dr. Weinberg. I did explain that this started in the town of Butland ZYX office with a man named Robert Smith and only him from the job. The man began by harassing me, then bullying me, then discriminating with witnesses, then threatening my job, and at the end of my job, I was getting sick with stomach pain and was finally dismissed for being sick. I have health problems that are primary and secondary. The primary symptoms are anxiety with all the conditions, IBS with cramps, pain, and diarrhea. The secondary is fibromyalgia, which affects the whole body in so many different ways; I asked the doctor if they knew about fibromyalgia problems and their effects on a patient body, and Dr. Weinberg said yes. There are more secondary of depression, psychosis, and others that I can't think of, but you said that you read my records, so you know all the information, then the doctor said yes, I know your symptoms from the records. I have doctors who say they understand my symptoms but don't want to cooperate with my attorney. Dr. Weinberg said that your doctors don't want to cooperate with your attorney and the courts; I said yes; Dr. Weinberg said that is unheard of and against state and federal laws.

Meanwhile, I have a town lying about me and the reasons for releasing me from my job. Then I have my attorney that family and I have caught in lies; I'm fighting everybody protecting the town from paying a settlement and being at fault. I spent about 11 years working hard as a sub-contractor with plowing to show I was good to work for the town to get a full-time job as an employee. The thing that blowout my mind was that this one man that I trusted turned against me in a heartbeat, and all the workers said that Robert was notorious as a boss. I said that at the time, I was 50 years old and had never had any problems like this or been released from any job in my life, and I think that is why this problem affected me the way it did with all the stress as well. The doctor said we were all done; I said that it was only about 45 minutes; the other doctor for the town took 2.5 hours. The doctor said I have read your records and talked to you, so I'm all set, I'll send the report to the court, and your attorney will receive it.

Two weeks later, I would call attorney Allen and ask about the two doctors' reports. Allen said that I had just received the court doctor's report; I asked about the town doctor's report, and Allen said yes, I have that one too. I asked about the town doctor's report. First, Allen said that he called you a fake altogether. I asked how I could fake my doctor or health problem with my doctor's answers and reports. Allen said I don't know, Vince. On the other hand, Allen said that the court doctor's report favors you and gives you 2.5 years of back pay from the town under workmen's comp. Pay. I said that would be wrong because I have fibromyalgia, a lifetime of problems and pain. Allen said you should be happy with what you just received from this doctor. I said we are in five years of fighting, and I see no end to this court. Allen would explain that we should receive a notice to go to court soon. I said that it would take about three months for a date. About a week later, after talking to Allen, I received a notice from the w/c court to be there on January 27, 2020.

I would go through my medical record from Dr. Rex Jax. This doctor was our independent personal doctor for our side, from attorney Allen. Dr. Rex was the closest to my price range to pay him for services, and Allen said he specializes in fibromyalgia. The price range was from $3,000.00 -

to $20,000.00. Unfortunately, I could not afford the highest doctor, but I believe you get what you pay for in services. But as I went through the report, the report was in favor of my cases. Still, it didn't have the related information on how the stress problems would connect to secondary problems related to the original stress problems. I would think of what Allen said about how Dr. Rex was a specialist with fibromyalgia. There was very little information about this fibromyalgia problem and how it related to stress problems. The report from Dr. Rex was ok, but he didn't have knowledge about fibromyalgia and stress-related problems. Therefore, the report didn't carry the proof we needed for the Workmen's Comp. Case. On the surface, the same problems with Allen sounded good, but underneath, Allen's talk and job performance were not suitable for an attorney. The worst part of the court ruling is that once the independent court doctor sends his report to the judge, all other medical records don't influence the judge, even if all the record says the same information. That includes the town doctor's disqualified report because of a time factor and laws.

I would get an e-mail from Allen asking me to set up a call appointment with him. We would set up an appointment just weeks before Christmas. The day came, and Allen explained that we should prolong the court date, and attorney Kerry also agreed to prolong the date. Allen would say that he needed to prepare for the court date, and attorney Kerry would also need the time. Plus, the fact of Christmas and I made plans to go away on vacation too. I said that between you and Kerry, canceling many dates and all the bull shit from all involved is crazy. I would bring up the fact that Dr. Rex didn't write a good report about fibromyalgia or stress-related problems. Allen said that it doesn't matter now with the court evaluation. All the other records don't count now, including that Kerry wants to disqualify the court evaluation herself with the judge. I said what!!! Allen said that he thinks it is because the senior judge said he wouldn't accept late documents. But that doesn't matter either because the court doctor has the last say in the case now.

I ask Allen why this woman is going out of her way to damage this case criminally. Allen said I don't know. I told Allen that I understand she has to fight for her clients, but when is it too much, primarily when she would lie about the facts? Attorney Kerry has been caught between us both and with my family with lies, the town's lies, and just about everyone not cooperating with the facts of the cases of lies. Once again, Allen said I don't know why you are going through all these problems with your cases. I told Allen you talk to this woman; you must see her intentions from her conversation. Allen said no; I said you must because when you take on a case must feel people out to see if they are lying to you or playing you a fool. Allen would say no. I said Allen, if you are in business for yourself, you must have ways of seeing problems; I did this with my business for all of the people I deal with customers, suppliers, workers, and just about anything that can go wrong with construction jobs. Again, Allen would say no. I saw that I wasn't making any good reasons with Allen, so I asked are we were all done. Allen would say no, I need an answer for the court to prolong the date. I said it sounds like the plan is already in place, so I have no choice with this answer, so yes, prolong the date again, Allen.

The date for January was canceled between the two attorneys for poor reasons. I have always noticed that nobody wants to work or do their job in the office when the holidays come. The way the government works and office workers push off work for as long as possible. It always has to be done yesterday when it comes to the physical labor jobs. I would receive a new appointment for the w/c office on March 26, 2020, another three months away. This time there would be a new development problem; this time, the original judge, Jill, would quit her job after January. Allen did not get the message to me right away, and then when I received an e-mail from Allen, I called him up and asked what was going on with this judge. Allen said that she quit and took back her application as a judge. I asked Allen if there was a conflict of interest with my case, and Allen said no. I said this looked funny and strange; I asked if she left for personal reasons, and Allen said no. I asked what happens now with the case, and Allen said we get a new judge. I then explained that we start all over with the new judge; Allen said yes. I asked whether we would need a new date; March would be canceled; Allen said no. When March rolled around, the world was in a panic with a virus; the virus was called covid 19. This would start in China, and it ran rampant across the globe.

This virus would change the world as we all know our world. The virus covid 19 was invented by our lovely governments and secret societies worldwide. Our world is overpopulated, and our governments thought of a way to cut the world population with natural causes or a virus. The sad part about death is no matter the cause of death; death never discriminates with any human, animal, or life form. But when you have a person or leader telling the people of the world that you are fighting for the right cause of life, this is the biggest lie from any government or leader. The world's governments and secret societies have a problem with the direct killing of people because the people of the world will revolt against governments and secret organizations. So that's why they all invented a virus, it's just like the black plague, but this was all-natural caused by fleas and rats of the European continent. Today's world has cleanliness that they did not have cleanliness and natural causes during the black plague time. These problems would be unheard of in today's world because of cleanliness. Our governments and secret societies are running our world right out of existence between wars that create nuclear, biological, and chemical warfare, and their waste contaminates our world. Now we have the viruses that our governments and secret societies with the scientific world of scientists who don't even know what they are doing to our world's population or the earth. The people of our world are suffering from leaders who are killing all of us. The part that doesn't make any sense is once all the ordinary people die, what are the rich, famous, and influential government leaders doing for common labor and other everyday lifestyles that they will have to do for themselves?

The virus would cause so much pain, hurt, confusion, loss of life, and insecurity. These problems happen when you have false governments and secret societies that run the world. The government lies and makes empty promises to the world's people, with one of the top leaders being the United States Government. There is another virus known as the American government. That has taken the land from the proper people of the American Indians. Our country was incorporated in 1776 to the present time, about 245 years. Our government has divided the people and conquered the people of America and many other countries over time. The government has put the young against the old, colors of people against each other, religions against each other, and many different situations. But the virus should have been the last straw that broke the camel's back. Our country has been shut down for about 2 years, from March 2020 to September 2022. We have many bad problems and consequences to our people of the world wearing masks to locking themselves in their houses, food shortest, and other household groceries with the economies all over the world failing from this virus. The children lost schooling time, which will have consequences now and in time. The country was divided by leaders hiding and stopping the world from life; the common workers were on the front line of the virus, trying to hold their jobs and help out the population. The virus problem will stop all the governments from doing their jobs and courts and justice for our country and the people. These consequences will lead to January 4, 2021, when the people are tired of a government that can't do their job right in any way, shape, or form; they are all losers in government offices. The list goes on forever and over time with all of the damage caused by this pandemic.

CHAPTER 29
Private Investigator

I would receive an e-mail from attorney Allen asking me have I had been working. I would show my mother and Jane my e-mail from Allen. All of us started to flip out with this information from Allen. I accuse the town and attorney Kerry of lies and a scandal to throw this case off its tracks. In other words, obstruction of justice and conspiracy of this case from Workmen's Comp. Office. I then told my mother and Jane this would be proof of tampering with the truth, evidence, and the facts of the case, and the facts of the town and attorneys fouling both cases' malicious intentions. I would ask Jane to record my phone call and have my phone on speaker so that my mother and Jane could listen and witness the conversation with Allen about these lies.

I called Allen, and he picked up the phone right away; I asked Allen calmly what was going on with the case Allen. Allen said that the town has you working for a company on videos and reports of them observing you working. I said what are you talking about, Allen. Allen asked if I saw the videos or reports, and I said no. I will send you the reports and videos. I asked Allen have you seen these videos and reports. Allen would say yes; I asked if he saw me in the videos. Allen said yes, I do. I then said I know you see a man in the videos but is it me or not, Allen would say yes again. That was all I needed to freak out with Allen. I wanted to kill him through the phone after what he said. I started yelling at him and said, " You been with me for six years, and you don't know what I look like or my face? And this would be the same for Kerry. I ask Allen if he trusts me. Allen said no, I said. I was thinking to myself to go along with this information from Allen. Then I said to Allen ok, Allen since you believe I'm the one in the videos, tell attorney Kerry to start a perjury case against me, and you can do the same. Allen said wait a minute; what do you mean? Wait. I said you believe that I'm in the videos, right. Allen said I'm not sure, Vince; I said it doesn't matter. The town attorney drums up this problem with lies. I want you to tell her to file charges against me, and we will deal with her problem of lies and prove that these two cases are lies from the beginning. Allen said I couldn't tell her that; I said I was admitting to working and the videos are correct. Allen said no, I could not do that. Allen would say you need to look at the videos and read the reports first. Why Allen, I know that I didn't work in any way, shape, or form for anybody. I don't need to prove anything to myself. I also have family members who can vouch that I have stayed in the house all day and night since this started in 2014. The most attorney Kerry would have from me going out is to my doctors. That would be all, Allen. Allen said to look at the videos and reports and call me back.

When I hung up the phone, my mother and Jane asked what the fuck was going on with this town attorney, Kerry, and Allen. I said this is how it's been from the beginning with everybody involved with the cases with lies. I asked Jane to try to get the videos up so we could see the truth of the lies. Well, Jane did that. I would print out the reports. I read the reports; I noticed two separate dates: November 24, 2019, and the second date was July 4, 2020. The company name was Professional private eyes inc., and out of Rhode Island.

The owner Pert Chanelle of the company, made the report for the attorney Kerry. The investigation company would have multiple employees at the scenes or places recording a man, a woman, and other employees from this company that were following me supposedly. The report stated how this company conducted its reports and received information about my family members and me. The company would look into Butland town hall for ownership of properties, registration of vehicles, and internet media searches. This company did its job almost right, but the problem was that they had the wrong people with false reports and videos. This company would find my brothers and sister, my mother and daughter, and my sister's boyfriend, Fred DeMello, who was the owner of a landscape company. The company stated that Vince had no vehicles in my name, and the last vehicle in my name was in 2017. I had a Facebook account with pictures of me, but with no new information, they would look up my business and find that the last time anything new was on there was in 2012. The company could not find me because I was always in my house with health problems.

Jane finally received the videos on Dropbox. Then, my mother and Jane sat and watched these videos of lies. The videos were real, but they had the faces of Fred, my sister Sarah, and other workers from Fred's company. Both videos were of Fred and Fred's company at work; this company's professional private eyes had the wrong people in these videos and reports. The worst part is that they looked up my Facebook media and had a picture of my face, and then this company lies in their reports and videos. My whole family and girlfriend freak out at the false allegations in these reports and videos. I started to think about the whole situation with w/c attorney Kerry and Allen and their little secret conversations when we were in court the last time. Then I explained to my family that these videos and reports were the secrets of the judge and attorneys who knew that an investigation company would be involved in looking for me and that I was being set up for failure when there was none to be. I then said that this is a conspiracy act of a white-collar crime. The plan was started by Kerry at court and then passed through the judge and my attorney Allen. My family and girlfriend said it sounded right that we saw them only in the courtroom and then said secret talk in front of us in the courtroom. The only problem is that I didn't have physical proof of this idea. Still, it was obvious that they all were talking around the investigation company with the town and attorney Kerry, judge, and attorney Allen's involvement which is a conspiracy act of a crime.

The next day I would call back Allen and say that I saw the videos and read the reports. I said to Allen that you believed that was me in the videos, and Allen said yes again, then Allen said that I wanted to withdraw from your case. I said what!!! Allen!!! If you do that, I will file a lawsuit against you and everybody involved in these cases. Something dirty is going on here with both cases. Then Allen said that Kerry wants your bank accounts, and she is going for a warrant for Fred's payroll accounts. I said that you and she were both wrong with all this information about me working. I said that you could see that it was not me, and according to the reports and videos, they were talking about my sister and Fred in the video and reports, not me. I said I don't have long hair and tits, Allen, and I'm not a heavy-set body Allen. I'm a skinny frame of a man with short hair and a goatee for facial hair, and there is nobody in the videos like that at all. Allen said Kerry wanted Fred's records from his company, and she is getting a warrant to do that. I also want to talk to Fred about this problem and hear from him that you didn't work for him; I said, OK, you could talk to Fred.

Fred would set up a time for Allen to ask him questions about me working for Fred. Allen would call my phone, and I would hand Fred the phone, and Allen would start asking questions about me. Fred said, " Let me explain before you start asking questions; Allen, I saw the videos and reports, and they are talking about me and Vince's sister Sarah in the videos and other workers. This investigations company picks up the two trucks in the driveway and follows them to my shop. Meanwhile, these two vehicles are registered to Sarah and me. These trucks have nothing to do with Vince, and as far as Vince is not working for me, that did not happen at all or at any time. I need to report any changes to my employees for insurance and employment laws and reasons. I'm not going to take a chance to break the laws and get in trouble. Allen said OK, you answer all my questions without asking, but Kerry still wants your and Vince's records. Fred said I have spoken to my attorney and my attorney said that I don't have to cooperate with this attorney Kerry or the town. Fred then said Allen, you are hurting Vince with your word games and legal games you are playing on him. Allen didn't have an answer for that statement from Fred. Finally, Allen would say OK, we are done with this phone call, Fred.

The next day after the phone call with Fred, I started copying my bank statement for Allen. Then I sent the bank statement to Allen by e-mail. Allen would respond to my e-mail by saying that you only have about $4.00 in the bank. I sent another e-mail saying that I hadn't had any money since the start of the problems in the town. I have no money at all, Allen. I ask Allen, what are you doing with the false accusations? Can we report these problems to the proper authorities, Allen? I would never get an answer to this question; I would think that Allen was hiding the truth from going forward for the better and justice. Attorney Kerry would send Fred the paper requesting his records. Attorney Kerry would also try to call Fred to talk with him without Fred's response. Allen would send an e-mail about the new judge Betty MacDuff. I would get the idea of writing an e-mail to this judge and explaining the problems of the two attorneys and the false reports and videos to her.

CHAPTER 30

Letter to the New Judge

I would start writing my first letter to Judge Betty Macduff, complaining about the entire situation of the case and attorneys that will be before your hearing date. I would also send the same letter to Senior Judge Bill Child for his input on the complaints and problems. My thoughts of exposing the complaints and problems of criminal acts from the Workmen's Comp case and the discrimination case are tied together with all these people involved in the two cases. This would allow two judges to take action together, finding the truth to all of the complaints and problems, and then take action on any criminal actions. In my letter, I explain that witnesses were being a cover-up, false reports from the beginning of this problem, starting with the town of Butland. False reports from two videos and written reports from attorney Kerry, with the knowledge of attorney Allen. Attorney Allen does not correctly represent his client; as an attorney of the laws, my rights as a citizen, the abuse from the town allegations, and two attorneys with false allegations from the cases. Plus, the facts of my health problems started with the town and now with no cooperation from everybody with my cases. There were also complaints about the previous judge earlier in the case, and questions about why she left her job and the case, knowing that the case would start with a new judge. I would think if something related to my case stopped her from continuing in the workmen's comp. office. I would give all this information and reassure them that I have proof and most of my records and videos to prove I'm telling the truth to them both. In return, the two judges would respond that this isn't the proper way of handling these problems, and you have an attorney to address these problems. Then, I would write an e-mail to both judges saying that the complaints, including my attorney as well as the whole case, were so bogus, and I needed help with my problems with the two cases and everybody involved.

Two weeks later, I received an e-mail saying that Judge Betty had sent my letter of complaint to Attorney Allen and Attorney Kerry. The excuse was that they needed to know everything going on with the case. I would also receive an e-mail from senior judge Bill saying that I can't get involved with cases. I would show my e-mails to my mother and family; my mother would explain that you are beating your head against a rock and you would not change the corruption in our laws and the people in charge as leaders. Unfortunately, you have a lot of bad luck with both of these cases, and it started with Robert, doctors, attorneys, judges, and all the lies that professional people said about you and the cases. My mother said you need to be careful about your health and health problems. We don't need anything more happening to you. I said to my mother that I was only fighting for the principle of the matter and the facts of the end of my life with my health, finances, jobs, and future in life. My mother would say to try to find another attorney to handle the case. I said yes, I would start calling attorneys.

The COVID-19 virus would affect my case with the w/c office and a lot of other cases throughout the country. Covid 19 would stop people from going to work, school, and just about everything. The only people who did work were essential people like the police dept., fire dept., doctors and nurses, food store people, etc. The courts were closed on all levels of courts, which made the process very difficult when crimes happened or any cases that were in the middle of their cases or new. Attorneys were hard to find because they would stay home with their families and close the courts. The world would be at a standstill for a long time. Things would slowly move forward in time, but my case would be held up with this virus for a long time. In time some court procedures would go to virtual meetings. The people who committed any crimes would be handled through the prison systems, and others would be handled through personal computers. My case was one of those virtual meetings when they happen or e-mails, where you are in the safety of your home, a person with any kind of court procedures it can be very stressful, especially when you are already having stress problems. One of my problems was an old computer, and I had to borrow an updated computer; then, being computer illiterate didn't help out with all the new technology in computers. This would also have an effect on the school departments with learning. The people who had new computers or old computers, smart with computers and illiterate with computers, who had computers power line and update power lines, then the apps or websites for virtual meeting and learning from schools. The problems would affect the middle class, poor people, and children with all this new technology.

When I started to call for attorneys, I would leave messages, and about 75% I would not hear from; the 25% would be split between those who took time to listen, and the others would say I'm not interested in the case. The ones who did listen to me would explain the main problem was that no attorney wanted to pick up a case with all types of problems. The attorneys would say that you are blackballed with your case; it sounds like intentionally, your case was doomed from the beginning because of the town. The doctors should have cooperated with your attorney, and then it's a question if your attorney did the right thing with the doctors. Now it's another question if the attorney is representing you for the better or worse; from how you explain your problems with your attorney, he neglects his powers with his client, and with the proof you have with the records, he will disbar him and put him in prison. The attorney would also say how the town attorney treats the case will also get the two town attorneys and your attorney disbarred for falsifying records. The judges knew that all the attorneys were doing things wrong with the cases. The attorney would also go back to the doctors by saying that all the doctors can be held responsible for their part of not revealing or holding back medical information on a legal matter and not cooperating. The therapy counselor can be held accountable for her action because she believed the computer, instead of her experience, that you would not hurt yourself or anyone else. Then the attorney went back to the judge and said that it's the judge's job to overlook the whole case and see when attorneys are abusing their powers and take time to listen to you as the people of the case. The attorney said that your entire case is bogus and that you need to start writing to your senators, D.A. attorneys of Suffolk County and Norfolk County, governor, attorney general, Justice Dept. in Sealand and Washington, F.B.I. in Sealand, and the news people to try to get your story out and then look for some justice in the process. Then the attorney said that this case was too big for me to handle; you need a large law firm to address all the different problems and areas involved with these cases.

I told the attorney that I had already sent letters to all the people you said. Nobody would help me with my complaints, and nobody answered, or they said it's not my job. The attorney said you need to keep after them; I said that anyone who makes a complaint should be taken seriously and not ignored. The attorney would agree and say that it's our government which is a big mistake with no one doing their jobs right in any way, shape, or form, then I agreed with him. The attorney said good luck with the heavy burden and said goodbye. I would come across some other attorneys who said the exact words as the first attorney. They all agreed with the simple fact that it's a shame what you are going through, but you need to argue the cases for yourself till someone will help you in the right direction of justice. They would say you have a more significant task than you know, and it's a shame at the same time what our government and laws are doing to the people of this country and around the world.

CHAPTER 31

Resending Letters

I would start writing letters again to all the proper law enforcement, legal authorities, and government authorities explaining my complaints of criminal actions involving my cases and the professional people handling my health and legal problems. I would never hear any response from anyone I wrote to these legal authorities. I wrote the first letters to the Rhode Island governor, and attorney general, F.B.I. Sealand office, four news media TV stations from Sealand, and the 2 Sealand newspapers. I would explain my health problems and my legal problems to the professional people handling my health and legal problems in my letters. I explained the start of the problems on how the town of Butland had wrongful dismissal of my job because of getting sick and was out of work with doctor's notes to cover any town's rules. The discrimination from Superintendent Robert Smith of the Butland ZYX office. The bullying, harassment, and threat to my job when I was sick from a stressful situation from, Superintendent Robert Smith.

Robert never explained why he dismissed me from my job, but after I retrieved an attorney, the lies began to come out after the facts from my being discharged from the town. Robert Smith would do anything to save their jobs and from a lawsuit. This man and town terrorized me for no reason, and they showed their power as bullies with lies and deceit. I explained that my doctors admitted I had stress-related health problems but would not tell the complete truth connecting it to my job and how bad my health would get over time. The doctors would not cooperate with my attorney Allen, laws, and the courts in any way, shape, or form. Now the problem of Attorney Allen is not properly defending his client as an attorney of law. All the lies that attorney Allen said and was caught lying with by my family and me. Allen was confronted with the lies he had just said. As an attorney, Allen would ignore situations altogether. All the information that I would pass on to attorney Allen and he would not use the information or look into the information I gave him, which would lead to neglect of an attorney. I also explained that Robert and the town, doctors, attorney Allen, and town attorneys would only add more stress to my health problems and life with all of the lies and confusion and changing my words of the original story and complaints.

I would take time to go and visit the offices of the F.B.I. in Sealand and Norfolk D.A. offices, file formal complaints about the whole story of my problems, and write my complaints in a letter to both offices. When I visited the F.B.I. office, it was like walking into a fortress with all the checks they do. When I finally spoke to an F.B.I. agent, he took my story of complaints, and he would also explain that Butland was under surveillance for other complaints. I asked what would happen with this complaint, and he said they would look into the problems, but I would never hear from them. When I visited the Norfolk D.A. office for the first time, they sent a couple of people to take my complaints, I explained the whole story to them, and they would be sympathetic to my complaints and problems but said that they could not help me with this situation. I asked where I go to have my complaints addressed with the results, and they weren't sure what office to go to for my problems. I would leave and say thank you to the people. When I got outside of the building, I said to Jane can you believe that the F.B.I. and D.A. offices don't help the people in any way, shape, or form, but they all want you to report crime and to cooperate with them, or you can be arrested for noncooperation with the laws. Jane said I know it's all conflicting information with our government and many more other problems with our government.

The second time is dealing with the Norfolk D.A. office; I would call asking them to talk to them and explain all the growing problems with all involved with these cases. At this point, the judges were added to the complaints and problems; all the letters that I was writing to the authorities were also explained in my letters. When I spoke to Assistant D. A. Attorney Sam Crow, I started asking if I could make a meeting to explain my problems, and I would have some of my records to show the proof of my problems. D. A. attorney Sam said that I need to make copies of the papers bring them in and drop them off with the secretary at the front desk. Then I will look over the information and call you back with a response and an answer. I would try to explain things, and Sam said you need to do this in a letter form and how I just explain the process. I would say ok to Sam and then ask how long will need to go over the papers, Sam said about a week, and I will call you. About two weeks later, I received a call from the D.A. office Sam . Sam explained that this wasn't something the D.A. office would deal with; I would ask where I go with my complaints and get results. I said that I tried everyone by writing letters with no response from them. Sam would say I know I read the information you sent; Sam said I have sympathy for you, but there is nothing I can do about this problem. Sam would say that you can try the Suffolk D.A. office in Sealand, where the courts are, and it is in her district. I would say ok, and Sam would say goodbye.

    I would also go to the police station in Butland and ask for assistance from them. When I got to the police station, the desk officer asked what I needed; I explained that I wanted to report the white-collar crime. The officer said I'll call someone to take your report. When the officer showed up, we went into a room, and he asked what I do for you; I said that I wanted to report a white-collar crime that started in 2014 to the present time with my job at ZYX office Butland with doctors, attorneys, and judges that don't have the truth from the attorneys. These doctors are not complying with attorneys judges, and courts. The police officer said you would need to report this to the Butland police. I said that's like going into the lion's den to report a crime in the same town, and I can't do that with my stress problems. I explained that my health problems would only worsen, like returning to the crime scene. A police officer said that where the problem started; another place you can report this is the Norfolk and Suffolk D. A. offices. I said that I live in Butland, and it also started here, where I live at the same time. The officer said that was the best I could do for you at this time. I said OK, that's fine. I'll take your advice and do that with the D.A. offices. Then I also thought of the state police in Milton and going there and reporting the crimes to them. When I got there, I would explain that I wanted to report a crime; the desk officer said I'll send someone out to help you. As I was waiting, I remembered that the state police deal with white-collar crimes on their website, which is why I was here trying another avenue. When the state police officer came out, we would go into a room, and I explained the problems and the officer said that I needed to go to the D. A. offices in Norfolk County. I said that your office deals with white-collar crimes, and the officer said yes, but it goes through the D.A. offices. Once again, I said OK, officer, I will do that and go to the D.A. offices. As I walked away from the police station, I was already at the DA office, and they said they don't deal with white-collar crimes.

I would write other letters to the Department of Justice in Washington D. C. for the reasons of their website stating that white-collar crimes will not be tolerated in our country. I would send two separate letters at different times and always got no reply from either letter. I would also send them letters by certified mail with the signature needed and all the other letters in the same way to all the offices that I wrote to explain my problems. One of the times of sending letters I would send letters to the Washington Post and the New York Times about my problems and complaints about an investigation. I would not get any reply from them either. Two signature cards didn't even come back from the Suffolk D. A. office and Washington Post in the last round of letters sent out. I would keep records of all my transactions, and it's amazing how a simple return signature card doesn't come back to me, Federal Mail, was tampered with these card's signatures. I would even write letters near the end of the workmen's comp. case; to two Rhode Island Senators. They claim they are here in the office to help the public in need of problems, and I didn't even get a reply from their office either. It's a sad day when a citizen tries to follow all the laws of this country, and nobody wants to deal with my problems of the crimes committed by me and the general public population of this country.

Government people and law enforcement people ignore a complaint from a citizen because it is against its kind or people of power, and regular people have no choice but to accept the screwing from our government and law enforcement. Unfortunately, I will not give up the fight for fair and equal life for justice for white-collar crimes and many other areas of crimes that the population has complained about for over many years. I have been educated that the pen is mightier than the sword in today's world, but in the old days of man's beginning, it was in the reversed way that the sword was mightier than the ink or pen. On the streets, guns are mightier than people, and this is how our government and law enforcement will treat us if it comes down to the end of fighting for our rights as citizens in our country. It is ironic. Military tactics are to divide and conquer the people. Still, our government is doing the same way to the public, for example, covid 19 and many other ways like many presidencies or legal offices that were altered somehow. What will come to our world with false leaders who lie and deceive and do anything they please to the world and our country?

I would bump into an old friend and attorney; we asked how things were. I said I was good, but I had a case giving me problems. Norman Lake said that was a shame; why didn't you call me first? I said I didn't think of you because of my health problems. Norman would say come by the office, and I'll try to help you with your case. I said OK, Norman see you tomorrow. So when tomorrow came first thing in the morning, I would go to Norman's office in Butland. I would walk in, and Norman would greet me and say, " Come in, please. We sat down, and Norman asked, explain your story. I would tell him the complete story from the beginning to the present. Norman said that you should have come to me first. Second, you can give me all the information from the discrimination case, and I will go through the papers and then give you an answer on what I found if it was legal or not legal. The cost will be about $1500.00. And I will look over the paperwork. I asked if he would be interested in the w/c case; Norman said no on a legal level, but I can and will help you along the way if possible. I asked why not on the legal side Norman said that you had two attorneys, and it sounded like the town was bribing them from the beginning, and then all the mistakes that were intentionally done wrong by the town and all attorneys.

You have a false letter from foremen and then false reports and videos showing you working. This was a setup; they had the judges in the pocket with this information, and you lost. You need to settle this case with money and get out for now. Then you come back telling your story without the proper channels of law. I said you want me to break the law? Norman said no. Norman said you would use the money to finance your story and book and get public support behind the book for an investigation on federal and state levels; without the feds or state having acted, you have no choice. So, if you have a computer, start writing. It will take time. Norman would say you came across a terrible situation with this town and all the attorneys, judges, and doctors. I have never heard of the plaintiff not being heard in court, never! I would say thank you, Norman, and go home.

CHAPTER 32
God and Religion

I would take time to think about how everything was unfolding for the worst in my life. I tried to follow the laws by writing letters and filing complaints with the proper authorities and received no results. I then started to think about the reports and videos about the lies that the town and attorney Kerry stated, with attorney Allen going along with their lies and Allen not fighting against the town and attorney Kerry's lies. I would start thinking that this could be a setup failing my case intentionally. If so, this would also be considered a conspiracy, malicious intentions, collusion, obstruction of justice, and many other legal terms applied to this problem. These words mean breaking the laws of this country and people's rights. I would try to show and prove that all the people involved with my cases are breaking the law and destroying my cases. I also said that there was a false letter from the foremen, and if we can prove that's a lie, then the whole two cases would be reopened for justice reasons. I would think that I had all the evidence and witnesses, and nobody wanted to hear about the laws being broken by the same people who enforced these laws. I would try another way of following our laws and writing to the new judge and the senior judge of the w/c office. I will try to show proof to the two judges with evidence and explain that witnesses are being covered up and have the truth.

I would write an e-mail to Judge Betty Macduff and Senior Judge Bill Child to explain that from the beginning of w/c with my discrimination case was being mishandled and criminal actions are needed. I explain how the town and all the attorneys are destroying the original complaints and story by manipulating my words, medical, legal, and cases. I said that I needed your help exposing the whole problem to everybody involved with these cases. I also explained that the attorneys implicated you, Judge Betty, and your office with Senior Judge Bill Child in criminal actions with my cases. I said that these attorneys have conspiracy, malicious intentions, collusion, obstruction of justice, and many other legal terms that would be applied to their criminal actions and my cases. I also explained that I was just trying to follow the laws with the procedures of reporting criminal interference from the town to the attorneys and doctors who have medical information on my health but will not admit it to my attorney or to the judges. Finally, I would explain that the two cases are bogus from the beginning and with everybody involved. I would give all of my contact information to get in touch with me, and we can resolve these problems.

About two weeks later, I would finally hear from the two judges. The Senior Judge Bill said that this doesn't happen in my office, criminal problems and you are not following the proper procedures, and you have a case judge handling the case and problems. Then I would open up the second e-mail with Judge Betty addressing me. It was also addressed to the senior judge, attorney Kerry, and attorney Allen. Judge Betty, explain that I am sending you Mr. D Angelo's email complaining about you and the case with its criminal information about the whole two cases. Mr. D Angelo said that witnesses are being covered up, the doctors and attorneys are covering up medical and legal information, and I am being implicated and my office in these problems; I will not tolerate these complications from anyone in my courtroom. Now, Mr. D Angelo, you will address all of the attorneys with your e-mails, and you will respect this courtroom and me as the Judge. The judge said that you have an attorney to handle your problems with him in person and not in my courtroom. I would show my mother and family the two e-mails sent to me by the judges. The family wouldn't understand that a man following the laws and reporting the crimes and getting the perception of being deceived by the judges when I asked for help in a court of law. Plus, all the people I asked outside of the cases said that the system and people are screwing me.

When my family heard and read these e-mails, they couldn't believe how the first judge couldn't handle the facts of a complaint in his office and look into the problems for himself that were complaining about his office. My family said they are pushing the problems off to avoid (cracks in the system) where there are no answers or justice for you. My mother asks me to sit down and calm down from the information. My mother said that you need to let this problem go because of your health and future health problems. It's not important enough to lose you because of your health problems. My mother said I know you will not back down from a legal or medical fight or anything else in this world, but you don't have a choice this time. I said thank you for caring mother and my family, but how will I take care of myself without a job, finances, or home; I have always paid my way in life, and if I borrow money, how will I pay them back? My mother said that your problem affects all of us in the process; you need to let go. My mother said that Lisa had told you to quit this case;

I said yes, and my mother said, OK, you have all the family saying the same thing. Mother said that you are also challenged by judges and attorneys with doctors and that this is a big mistake you are making; you can end up in jail for disputing the laws, legal people, and doctors. I said to my mother that I would not go to jail for disputing the things of the law; I would be fine. I said that's why these professional people get away with breaking the laws and bullying the common people; they give up being afraid of the consequences. Nobody in this world should ever be afraid of anyone or anything for many reasons. I said that I just needed someone to hear the complaints in the original way of explaining to them that's all mother. If the original complaints are wrong, I will give up, but I'm not wrong with my knowledge about my rights as a citizen.

I will send another e-mail response to the judge's answer to my previous e-mail. I said in my e-mail that I sent you a whistle-blowing letter about the whole case that you and the senior judge are handling and with information about my other case. In return, you turned my e-mail to the attorneys that I was complaining about and with me blowing the whistle on them. I was asking for help from you judges regarding criminal actions that are happening with my cases and could incriminate both judges in the problems the attorneys started, and this is how you pay me back. I was very disappointed with you and the senior judge lying to protect criminals in your office. I would never get a response from either judge with this complaint to them and how they handle a whistle-blowing letter about my cases. For the time being, I would let it go for now.

When I received more information about false reports and videos and that Allen wasn't doing anything about this new problem, I got mad. I would then write another e-mail explaining the problems about the false allegations of reports and videos and the conduct of my attorney and the town attorney, Kerry. I would explain to Judge Betty that Attorney Kerry presented false reports and videos of me working with Attorney Allen. When I saw it, it was videos of my sister Sarah and Fred with his workers. The two attorneys know my face and the investigation company because of social media pictures. I saw the videos myself, and I believe that this is an attempt to sabotage my case with you, Judge Betty; this is the same thing that the discrimination attorney Gram did with a false letter from Foreman Scott. I would like to know what you will do with these lies and the problem. When I finish the e-mail, I will send it to all of these people: Judge Betty, Attorney Kerry, Attorney Allen, and Senior Judge Bill. I would never hear anything about this e-mail from anyone; it's like they just avoided the e-mail. Once again, this is criminal action now involving judges with workmen's comp's office, I received an e-mail from the Senior Judge Bill stating that this problem doesn't happen in his office. The funny thing is that the town's attorneys play the same trick in a court of law; one time was a letter from Foreman Scott, and then the other two times with false reports and videos of other people. Meanwhile, as the covid 19 was running rampant, I would ask when we would have a hearing date. I wouldn't get an answer from these e-mails again.

Attorney Allen would send in a motion to drop out of the case multiple times; this time was within legal procedures. We would have another video hearing about Attorney Allen dropping the case. Attorney Kerry would send in all types of Motions saying that her clients are upset with this new development. Her clients have spent all kinds of money to defend these cases, and they want it to stop; Attorney Kerry would also ask for a dismissal of the case again. The judge would say we will set up a video meeting to resolve this problem. We would get a notice by e-mail within a week. The day came for the meeting. I was the first one online for the video meeting, then the judge's secretary, then Allen, who explained he was on vacation at the time again, and then Kerry, who forgot about this meeting. After we all checked in, the judge came online, and she asked

Allen to present his motions. Allen would explain that his client wrote the e-mail letters complaining about my services, and I believe that my client wants to represent himself instead of an attorney. If I continue to represent my client, it could incriminate me with these two cases. The judge asked Kerry what about your motions; Kerry said, my clients and I want you to dismiss the case, and the judge said, no, I would not do this dismissal.

Kerry said that if you grant Allen's request to drop out of the case, this case will have to continue until Mr. D Angelo retains a new attorney. If you allow Mr. D Angelo to represent the case, the man is not stable or capable with his mind or mental problems. Judge Betty said that I see he can write interesting e-mails, so I think he is capable of handling his side of the case, but representing as an attorney is another problem because he does not know the laws. Allen would interrupt and say, judge, my client is capable mentally, as you said, writing the emails, Mr. D Angelo has a stress problem, and he isn't a violent problem, just that he gets sick from the stress problems. Then Mr. D Angelo has to be rushed to the hospital, which could hold up the case. The judge asked me whether I had anything to say. I said yes, I do; for a start, you haven't addressed my claims to you about my emails explaining all the problems from before in the e-mails, and I know these false reports and videos are a bigger problem.

Meanwhile, Allen wants to drop out because it will incriminate him with my cases; this only shows that my attorney is guilty of representing me. We have a town attorney who started all these new problems with false reports and videos and then called me crazy when it was only stress-related problems. Are you kidding me or what? Judge Betty said I would take this under advisement, and I would have an answer in a week at which another video meeting would happen.

We had a video meeting with Judge Betty, Attorney Kerry, Attorney Allen, and me one week later. Judge Betty started talking first about Allen's motion, and she agreed with Allen dropping out of the case. Kerry went to say something, and the judge stopped her and said you, Kerry is, going to deal with this as-is, with Mr. D Angelo representing himself. I don't know about these other problems, but we are going forward with a hearing date when we all have a clear from covid 19 of going back to work as the courts. But for now, we will have to wait for an answer from our governor when we can start court. Judge Betty asked Kerry whether there was anything else to hear. Kerry would say no, judge.

Mr. D Angelo, are you getting an attorney to deal with this court case? I said no because I've been trying way before this date and had no results in obtaining an attorney to replace Allen. Judge Betty said that I would strongly stress hiring an attorney for this case for workmen's comp. Case. I said I tried with no results; Allen would interrupt and tell the judge that Mr. D Angelo has a right to defend himself. The judge said I wanted an attorney. It is too difficult for a citizen to try this case. I told the judge I didn't want this to end as a long wait to get to a hearing. The judge answered well, you lost your attorney. I want you to have a new attorney; I ask about the e-mails and whether you will deal with the questions from them. I said that this is sabotage of my case from attorney Kerry and now with you, judge. I said I know you will drag this case forever; the judge asked if I was done, and I said yes. The judge said you would give me an update by e-mail for attorneys.

I would send an e-mail letter to the senior judge complaining about the case judge and her actions during court meetings. I explained to a senior judge that I wrote e-mails to you and the case judge about the activities of attorneys and doctors along with all the corruption involved with my cases. Your e-mail response was that this didn't happen in your courtroom and office, but this is a lie, especially when I was showing evidence and telling you. Now we have false reports and videos of me working. I want to know what you are going to do with this information. The next day I received an e-mail from the senior judge saying that you were harassing me and Judge Betty with your e-mail letters. I can put in a complaint against you for this crime. The senior judge said you have an attorney to deal with these problems. If you keep on harassing the judges, I will call for an investigation into this matter and press charges. I would receive the e-mail from the senior judge, read the e-mail, and start to go on the rampage in my room. Finally, I was so piss-off that I wrote back and started to go ahead and report my letters to the cops. I don't care; maybe I will get justice then when other people (police) hear the problems I have been complaining about for years. Then you can be judged by your peers in court to see how you like these problems. Then I would send the e-mail to the senior judge. In the following e-mail, the tune was better from the senior judge but didn't address any of the problems I expressed to him or case judge Betty. In other words, all were ignoring all my complaints on all levels and with each other.

CHAPTER 33

Mental Abuse and Fibromyalgia

The people of this country complain about physical abuse and mental abuse. Physical abuse is very noticeable in many ways, and nobody can deny these facts. But when it comes to mental abuse, people will always deny these facts. The scary part of our country and people is that we all give mental abuse to each other intentionally and accidentally, and sometimes the person doesn't even know that they are hurting the other person. The common knowledge of areas where this mental abuse happens and begins is our 1st families, 2nd workplace, 3rd disabled people or people that are different, 4th racism, age, cultures, nationalities, and many other areas. We should all be ashamed of any physical and mental abuse to our people like 1st mothers and fathers, 2nd adults and children, 3rd bosses and workers, and just like everyday people. Unfortunately, we live in a world of abuse from every angle possible, and many people get hurt every day from all types of abuse. The problem of abuse starts with the president as the teacher of the world, and then it rolls through all the branches of our government. The abuse enters businesses and follows the parents of a child or children that are the only innocent ones here, that get abused with no answers of justice, even animals. Russia is the best example of the worst at present. But the rest of the world that stands by and allows the ignorance of killing innocent men, women, and children should face the same consequences as Russia. We are in the year 2022, and our government says that we are civilized people, but it shows that we as a world are not civilized. People worldwide are being abused, being in the war with Russia, directly fighting for their lives and rights; well, other people are watching the war on the sidelines showing the abuse. War will always affect all the people of the world in some way. Wars are evidence of physical and mental abuse. Plus, the facts of teaching people that war is OK with all the abuse and loss of life and lifelong trauma. We as a world should never allow wars to come to our lands or our world. This should be outlawed forever in all the countries of our world.

When I started my business, I noticed that I was a leader, and I had to handle customers, suppliers, and workers, with some type of care for people, plus knowledge of the work of construction. I would always learn that it takes a strong person to be in charge of other people. As a leader, you cannot make mistakes in business; when you make mistakes, people can get hurt or die or lose their homes and belongings. The most incredible honor in our world is when people trust you and believe in you, in my case building and construction work. It takes a lot of hard work and knowledge to build anything, including a world, but it isn't easy being a leader where you would have to look out for everybody on the job. The workers were always a challenge because of drinking, drugs, poor work habits, and who could be trusted. I would be the leader and teacher of the proper way of conducting myself with my surroundings, setting a good example for people to follow. Unfortunately, when it comes to people like our government who are at the top of setting the best examples, the government fails with flying colors. Our government is the one to stop all our country's problems, and they choose the divide and conquer technique. The history of our time in this country shows how our government has led the people in disarray of confusion and disorder, and the government's laws show more proof of failure.

We have all types of information about the abuse but have no answers to resolve the answers or questions. We have commercials for mental abuse and that people should go and get help for their mental problems. When a tragedy happens, like a school shooting, they offer therapy counseling. Like the Sealand bombing, the government provides therapy counseling which is a good start to helping the people. Now we have the doctors that we visit, and the doctors only want to prescribe drugs to handle a person's mental problems. The doctors don't look at the whole picture of a person's life; a person's life revolves around work, family the safety of others. My doctors said here is your prescription, and go to work; I would say that I have to go to work with this medicine in my body and for the safety of the people in question and me. The doctors would say that you have to deal with this problem, not me. I would explain that my body system is dizzy and headaches, and you want me to take a drug that my job wouldn't allow on the job. The responsibility between me and a job would be to neglect on my behalf; it is irresponsible on my behalf and on the doctor's behalf to be irresponsible and neglectful. This problem is considered abuse of doctors and doctors' neglect, leading to malpractice lawsuits and jail time. Then you have to find an attorney to handle the problems that a doctor did of neglect to their patient. Then the attorney gives you a bullshit story that you can't prove in court, which is also another part of legal neglect and abuse. All of this is because, in Rhode Island, professional people don't go against each other in any way, shape, or form. Professional people (politicians, attorneys, judges, doctors, etc.) protect each other at all costs, including their people's lives and family members' lives. Once again, the government has the power to stop all of this abusive activity, and the government allows the abusive problems to continue at all costs, and the price is money.

Mental disorders are about 200 different types of mental disorders. The common ones are a category with more information under the titles: anxiety disorders, dissociation disorders, mood disorders, trauma, and stressor-related disorders, neuro-developmental disorders, sleep-wake disorders, neuro-cognitive disorders, and substance-related and addictive disorders, and the lists go on forever. Some of these disorders are babies born that way, and it is a question of how these problems may happen. Then you have the people starting from a child to adults that use street drugs and medical drugs. Then you have people who go to war or live in their country with war (Ukraine) with problems. You also have conditions with a boss or co-workers that give you hard times for no reason. I would fall under these answers from my research with my computer when people play head games like a boyfriend or a girlfriend or just from work, family, and many other ways. Then you have professional people who play head games as well; I would fit under some of these problems. The doctors couldn't figure out the problems with me, but I did, and when I confronted the doctors, attorneys, and judges, they didn't like my answers. So now they intentionally foul my cases and my mind and body. The officials and people don't understand retaliation and revenge for a person's life that got destroyed by problems from another person or, worse, our government. That leads to these circumstances of a tragedy for that person.

The problem with fibromyalgia is that information that the doctors don't want to tell the people or patients or even admit on the record is how dangerous this fibromyalgia can get in a human body. Remember that the

C.D.C. has all the information in their medical books or websites where I got my information, and doctors deny me the answers that I received from the C.D.C. office. When it came to my attorney Allen and the information from the C.D.C. office, attorney Allen said that it didn't come from a doctor. The notice from the workmen's comp. office, the w/c office states in their paperwork (please bring with you all medical reports and other documentary materials you will be relying on) to court. Still, attorney Allen said that this information doesn't apply to you in any way, shape, or form. When the COVID-19 pandemic hit the world, the officials from the C.D.C. office had medical control over our government and worldwide. Meanwhile, I have an attorney telling me the notice from the w/c office doesn't matter, and the C.D.C. office doesn't matter either.

The causes of fibromyalgia are stress-related problems such as; anxiety, depression, IBS (irritable bowel syndrome), psychosis, panic attacks, PTSD (post-traumatic stress disorder), the nervous system, some kind of a tragedy, nerve damage after three years of having fibromyalgia, etc... In addition, there are secondary problems, along with the main problems; such as sleep disorder, different types of pains, daze and confusion, fogginess, hard time breathing, headaches, chest pains, joint pains, muscle pains, and nervous system compromise, etc.

What kind of conditions would contribute any person to these medical problems and mental problems conditions; tragedy is when a boss bullies himself on a person or people, boss harasses a person or people, boss threatens a person's job for no reason, boss lies about the whole story, a false letter from a foreman, all attorneys covering up the truth and witnesses, doctors that admitted stress-related problems but didn't place blame to the proper person or people, writing letters and complaints to proper authorities with no results or answers, writing to judges with complaints about all attorneys and just ignored the complaints, whistleblowing to a judge about attorneys then gave my information back to the attorneys, writing to the news media to investigate my complaints with no response. The worst part of all these facts is that I try to follow the laws to their fullness without losing everything in my life. The laws and authorities can break their laws, but a citizen can't do the slightest thing wrong without going to jail. So the odds are stacked against the citizens of America.

The results of fibromyalgia can be devastating to any person who has fibromyalgia. All of my research on medical and legal information shows and proves that I know more than professional people. I only have a high school education and some trade colleges, plus the experience of having medical problems. The wonderful thing about technology is the facts you can find on the internet and use against the people who make the laws and enforce the laws. The internet is better than the reference law books that they refer to for cases. You can catch the lies from all involved with a case or cases. This also works for the medical information with your doctors and their bullshit stories of I don't know what's wrong with a patient. The internet knows the truth about a lot of information when you can look it up on the internet. The medical information about fibromyalgia at the end is; loss feeling of in your feet and hands, pains in all your joints, nervous system failure in time, and spinal pain, which brings on headaches and the daze, confusion, and fogginess in your mind; it can affect your muscles or deteriorates your muscles over time, and were your nervous system connects to all your major organs, and much more can have problems too. The way I see things in a human body is that there are two main lines in your body; 1 is your bloodline, and 2 is your nervous system. The blood is for oxygen, and the nervous system controls your body parts and muscles. Without those two system lines in your body, nothing else will work in your body.

CHAPTER 34

Standing Alone

I would be standing alone when attorney Allen quit my case, and Judge Betty allowed his quitting. Attorney Allen would have often left me standing to deal with all his mistakes and not fight for me as an attorney. Meanwhile, I was like David and Goliath in the bible against a state judge Betty of Workmen's Comp. Office and attorney Kerry, two against one. Incredibly my chances had diminished since I had no attorney, and the judge was playing the rules of law against me with attorney Kerry. I would e-mail Judge Betty a month after Allen quit, explaining to Judge Betty that I had to look for an attorney to take the case, and no attorney wanted the case. It was also complicated with the covid 19 in place with attorneys. The stress level within me was so high, and the pain was incredible throughout my body; 7 years later, I fought the same problems from a town and attorneys with doctors and judges and all the problems created by all the people involved with my cases. I would try to push through this case, Judge Betty and attorney Kerry, and I would try to prove the lies from the town and attorney Kerry. I would also show that Attorney Allen did not do his job right in any way, shape, or form. Officials with power can change the outcome of anything with their powers and with lies and corruption. It would be considered the squeeze play from two ends to make you do what they want, even if against the laws.

Judge Betty would eventually answer the e-mail and say that a hearing date is out of her control and she doesn't make the dates for a hearing. I thought it was pretty funny that a judge, Betty, would say these words that she had no control over dates when we were in court; she and any other judge would say, I'll see you in a week, a month, or six months. The lies from all these people are so incredible that they just blow out my mind. But when you show the truth and the laws that apply to your case and the people involved, just ignore it or overrule your answers to avoid the situation. The problems are the same with attorney Allen or myself. You get the run around with no results, good or bad; in my case, it's all bad. Once again, I would write an e-mail to senior judge Bill complaining about a hearing date. We had video conferences, and dates were made on time, but to get a hearing date was like pulling teeth from a stubbing animal. The sad part is that the animal is a human being who intentionally stopped the process of court procedures and due process of justice. I would eventually hear from senior judge Bill, and he said that you need to stop bothering this office. Once again, senior judge Bill would threaten me with calling the cops and reporting this problem of your complaints of harassing judges. I would not get a proper response from the senior judge Bill. Still, I would respond to his e-mail saying that if you consider me harassing you and the case Judge Betty, I said to imagine a boss harassing a worker, discriminating, bullying workers. If you like, I have no problems with the police getting involved with this matter at all, Senior Judge Bill.

The problem with anyone calling the police would lead to an investigation to see if any criminal issues needed the attention of criminal actions. Then maybe the truth would shine through and resolve the complete problems with everybody involved with these two cases.

Unfortunately, nobody would call the police on incriminating themselves with two cases, and all the professional people. I got the run around with everybody from the start, which was Robert Smith and the town of Butland. All the doctors were not cooperating with my attorney and the courts. With all false documents and letters, false reports and videos, then many lies to cover up witnesses and all of the truth to the ignored facts. Robert would start altering the complaints, and then attorneys would change the original complaints from me to their complaints of lies that had no truth or value under our laws. In other words, each one of them intentionally and maliciously falsified and failed our laws and the two cases in their way. Now we have the judges who did the same, deliberately and maliciously deceiving the laws and justice. We do the people go for justice and order with a corrupt law system, federal, state, town leaders, etc. I would think about how to try to follow the laws that have so much controversy within our laws and order, people, government, greed, power, pain, and hurt countries individually and as a world. What will it take to straighten out our world for the better, an act of God or worse, World War Three with a nuclear bomb? The extinction of man, woman, and children and all that lives on our earth. What is left but chaos when we lose all hope of laws and order and government? We saw chaos in motion with the capital riots on January 6, 2021. It is only the beginning of what is to come with our government and our future as a world. We lost the foundations of government and society throughout the world because of greed and power. The world should put down their ignorance and work together for the best of everyone in the world equally and united together.

The rich and powerful people are the poison of our world with their way of power and greed. Here would be the problem of my two cases, between the town and attorneys with doctors and judges. These people can deliver justice or take justice away. It all comes down to the individual's thoughts with the power to follow the laws and order. In my cases with Robert and the town with attorneys, doctors, judges, senators, governor, attorney general, F.B.I., Justice Department in Washington D.C., Norfolk and Suffolk D.A. office and news media. Where does a person report abuse from our law system that doesn't want to hear the problems? My friend, attorney Norman Lake said all you can do is write a book about your problems so that the world can know how badly you were treated by our legal and medical systems and other related systems. Norman would also say that we lost all respect for each other as people in our country and world. I would get no respect as a citizen defending myself from the attorney and judge. At the same time, you have to defend yourself without the respect of the attorneys and judges at the time in court. We have law books that make it very difficult to get a copy of these books and to find these books as a common citizen is also difficult. We also have law books of references with all types of old cases referred to when presenting cases, but the attorneys and judges use the references as laws when the references are not. Every case is an independent case with similarities, but the difference outweighs the problems of that independent case reference. It is only made into books for a similar ruling from past cases, the only time this reference may change is if the reference turns into a bill and then is approved by Congress and the Senate. In our country, lawmakers and law enforcers turn laws and order into their interpretations of the laws and order. The system will break down, and people will revolt against our government and any government that breaks its laws and order. Capital riots happened on January 4, 2021, with our government saying that it is against the law to attack our government. But this has happened to our country's citizens from the beginning of our government throughout our time. Especially from 1776 to the present time in our country being born (245 years) ago. And with our two presidents, Abraham Lincoln and John F. Kennedy. The people have the right to question our government without any consequences to the people.

Unfortunately, our government does have consequences. It's called a betrayal of our country, and it is a jailable offense and much more. It's no different from not listening to the judge; this is called contempt in court and is a jailable offense. Good citizen challenges the courts or governments and is heard with a proper answer from the judge or government to the people without consequences. How can I challenge Judge Betty and Kerry to follow the laws and prove that my complete cases were fraud from the beginning without the abuse of the laws and orders from the attorney Kerry and Judge Betty? The judge and attorney would drag my case out for many months in 2021. Then, I would see attorney Norman and talk to him again about the case, and Norman would say, I told you to try to end the case with a settlement and then write a book about your story and try to recover your losses from the book. I would explain that I have the proof and question all the problems in the case. Attorney Norman said you couldn't fix the broken system, and the odds are against you in so many ways. Norman said to settle the case the best you can, start writing the book, and let the people know about the problems you faced for seven years. I would say, ok, Norman. Then I went home to try to settle the case. I would write an e-mail to Judge Betty explaining that the town has offered me a settlement of $35,000.00 repeatedly over time. We had an agreement with the town and attorney Kerry that they denied after with the mediation judge of $50,000.00.

When Judge Betty received this e-mail, she would answer the e-mail within an hour of sending it. Judge Betty said that she knew nothing of any settlement talk from either side of the attorneys. Here is another time that attorney Allen was lying about not notifying the judge about the settlement. Judge Betty would say that she would look into this issue. Judge Betty asked in her e-mail why she was trying to settle this case now and not taking the case to a hearing. I would reply with an e-mail and an answer that everybody involved with this case has done wrong with all of the information legally and medically. I have lost everything personal, material, and family, and my health is failing more each day with this case and the other case I lost, as I explained before to you in e-mails. I would receive another e-mail from Judge Betty asking me if I still wanted to settle this case by the end of the day. If I was serious with the settlement of the case, with the town of Butland and attorney Kerry would only agree with the settlement of $35,000.00 and not be responsible for the case and claim. We will set a hearing time if you agree with these terms. I would send an e-mail explaining that I would agree with the terms. A date would be set up for a hearing with another e-mail a week later.

I would go to my mother to explain the news about the case, and it was settled. My mother said that this was a good thing to settle and maybe get better with your health without the stress of the case. I said that attorney Norman said to settle the case and write a story about the problems that I went through. My mother said it's good to do it, especially when you have health problems. You can take your time and write about all the people and problems of your cases. Then I said it didn't feel right with my heart and mind to settle. It's like the town and attorneys got away with beating down me and laws with power, money, and lies. My mother would say that the town is paying for the problem of lying. I would say this is a one-time payment for the rest of my life; what do I do after? My mother said you take Norman's advice, write the book, and see where it takes you. My mother said you might be shocked by the results of the book meaning good things. I would start writing the book to explain my side of the story to the public without the lies.

One week after the e-mail to Judge Betty, we would have a video hearing with Judge Betty, attorney Kerry, and me. During the meeting, Judge Betty explains the circumstances of the hearing with the town of Butland and Vince D Angelo of a settlement. Judge Betty explained that I would not be able to proceed with any arguments once we have an agreement. Judge Betty also said that the town would not be responsible for any future problems in the future of this case. Judge Betty said that the agreement was for a settlement of $35,000.00. Do you agree with all the information I said, Mr. D Angelo? I said yes, and I agreed with the terms of the settlement. Judge Betty asked Attorney Kerry if she understood the settlement agreement terms; Attorney Kerry said yes. Judge Betty said that I grant these terms of a settlement. Judge Betty asked, are there any questions for the parties involved? I said that there is a lien against this case with the state of Rhode Island (state health insurance). Judge Betty asked the attorney, Kerry, do you have this information from the state. Attorney Kerry said that there is a difference of $1,029.00. Judge Betty said that the town would cover that problem, and Attorney Kerry said yes.

Then I ask how long it will take to receive a check. Attorney Kerry said that the laws were two weeks after the judge signed them. Then Kerry said I would need more time for Mr. D Angelo to receive a check from the town. The judge asked how long to attorney Kerry, and she said about four weeks. I said that I waited seven long years for a check, and they are asking for more time; that's incredible. Judge Betty said can you get this done sooner to the attorney? Kerry said I'll try with the town. Judge Betty asked if there were any more questions. I said yes; I have one more question why didn't this happen with the $50,000.00? Judge Betty said that it was a different matter that wasn't agreed upon in the proceeding from before. Judge Betty would close the video hearing. I would wait just after four weeks, and I had no check. I would e-mail Judge Betty saying that I haven't received a check. I said that the law says two weeks, and you granted attorney Kerry four weeks and still have no check. Can I receive penalties and interest? Judge Betty would look into the problem and receive a payment notice to me within the next month. Another month later June 26, 2021, I received a check from the town of Butland and the end of workmen's comp. Case. Now I start the writing of the book and the problems of writing the book only, not knowing if the book will succeed or the process of publishing a book.

CHAPTER 35
The Challenges

The challenges of writing a book are incredible in so many ways. It's better to have the education, knowledge, and learning of any new career choice. I went to school for carpentry and construction and learned over the years of working in my field. I was led to write this book differently, but I never learned how to write anything professionally. I started out writing love letters when I was a young adult and then writing estimates and contracts for customers; at one time, I wrote a diary for six months, and then I wrote a book in the year 2008, which led up to this book. Writing my book lets the public know the criminal actions that happened to me and have or could happen to others. White-collar crimes are the beginning of crimes done in our country and world. It is a plot to harm, hurt, destroy, and many other situations; this would lead to people, companies, politicians, police, government, and anything there for the taking. The sad part of our country and world is that nobody cares about each other. It's all about the power and greed of an individual or groups of people. One man with power ruined my life, and then a town is backing up a liar, and then a town avoids their responsibility of being wrong and the responsibility of settlement which comes down to the money.

The challenges of dealing with my health problems as well as when I was writing this book were incredibly difficult to deal with at the same time. When I started, I gathered all my legal records, medical, e-mails, and memory and referred back to the records as needed. The difference between a story fiction is the writer's imagination compared to a non-fiction story, which has the truth and reality of the true story, which was very difficult for a beginner writing his first true story. I would find the proper words best to describe this story's facts, problems, and situations. I would also write directly to explain the story without all the technical words and terms, basically a simple form of a story. I would also make up a name list for the book and for me to remember the characters in the story, unlike the real names of the people involved. I would also need a dictionary for the words I couldn't spell, and I was not a good typist who would take longer to type the book. I would watch the news with their articles and add in the reality of everyday problems from the news and other sources. I would also use T.V. commercials about medicines and abuse, which were also on the television. I would remember all the information for my book to be written, juggling all of my information to write this true story.

When I started writing this book, I didn't know if I would do a good job writing. I knew that the storyline would be a hot topic to write about, but choosing the right words to explain it was another situation. I always want to change my career from being a carpenter/construction worker to something that I use my mind and not a physical job. When I ended up with my health problems from my job with the ZYX office in Butland, I never thought I would be writing my life story of a tragedy. I would think of writing science fiction stories, not true-life stories. Writing this story brings out so many emotional feelings about how I went through things. It was like reliving all of my problems over and over again. I would go through the emotions of rage, hurt, the pain of losing, failing as a man, and many other deep feelings. It wasn't easy to show my feelings in words and write about them in my book. The flashbacks of being taken advantage of and being so vulnerable without my job. At the same time the facts of writing about my feeling and the truth about what happened with my complete story. These are my feelings that I never had to explain; I was always in a positive direction with my own business and lifestyle. Unfortunately, life goes through changes whether we like it or not. My life would change over seven long years multiple times with each up and downs of this case and each individual that I had to deal with, for better or worse.

When I had to read the medical and legal records, it was challenging because of the lies in these records. My original story and complaints were changed so many times that I couldn't believe it. Once the information was on paper and in the documents that all professional people would see, nobody questioned why I was fighting very much and had to straighten out the records. When it came to my research with medical and legal information and sized it against my medical and legal documents on record, it was night and day or day and night. These records had no similar information at all. The record information only made sense with their lies, not my original complaints and story; this would include medical and legal records. It is unfortunate how far people will go to distort and deceive the accurate information in these two cases. This would lead my thoughts to how many more people had the same lies done to them, and nobody cared about the truth in our country.

As I wrote the story, I would get sick trying to think about what did happen throughout my story. I would have a hard time sitting, standing, walking, and lying down. The more complicated part was going through my thoughts and paperwork because it brought all the problems again. My fibromyalgia, PTSD, and anxiety with all of its side effects would start acting up, and I would have to stop my writing. Remember that my cases were all finished, and the symptoms would attack me just by writing and explaining my story and complaints, which would make things very difficult with writing and the everyday things I had to do for myself. Hearing information from the news media, commercials, and documents is so contradictory to how the doctors, attorneys, and laws work are just bull shit lies with our overall systems. The real criminals are the ones that have too much, compared to the poor who have nothing but problems from the ones. The actual story is a bad roller coaster ride, but writing the novel was worse than any nightmare.

CHAPTER 36
The Media

I would write letters to the newspapers and the four news stations around Sealand. I wrote to them for them to investigate my story and the complaints. I would never hear from anyone from any newspapers or news stations. I have written multiple letters multiple times to all types of official people asking for an investigation and help with my need for justice. The news people ask for tips about news information, just like the police use the news to find criminals through the media with public help. When a person asks for help from the news media to do their investigation and expose problems, they are nowhere to be found. And the same could be said about the police. The funny part of these two establishments is that when a person or people cry out for justice, where are they when a person or people need their aid? A problem like this is on a physical level; when it deals with the white-collar crime level, they don't even look at the issues or problems of complaints. Then when the people take things into their own hands, that is when it is against the laws of this country. The problem is that the people are only defending their lives because the proper authorities ignore the first complaints of a person or people. Then when the news people get the story, the story gets cut up in so many ways that it is incredible. The news media is only interested in rating; they don't stand up for the rights of accurate news information and the people. Our lovely authorities and government tell the news media what to say and print, and these officials censor the news. When a citizen writes to the news media complaining about our government, they tuck tail and hide and reject the story from that citizen or me. There is an old saying that "the one outweighs the many, and sometimes the many outweigh the one." These are complex problems that people will have to face; the problem is that this would only apply to the powerful, rich, and greedy ones of our world. The poor have no chance, unlike the other people that I just explained, the poor are always expendable in so many ways, and our history shows the truth.

Rhode Island has its share of criminals and our country, the United States, and worldwide do as well. One example is 9/11/2001. The news was all over the Twin Towers in New York City, and we all saw the tragedy of that day. Another time was in Rhode Island with James's "Whitey" Bulger made news multiple times with F.B.I.; the F.B.I. was asking for help from the public to give tips about his whereabouts in our world. Also, the Sealand bombing from the marathon race and the chase of the brothers. These crimes were the physical side of the crimes; there is another side to planning a crime and acting upon the crime. The planning of any crime is the crucial point of executing the plans. White-collar crimes have many names like; conspiracy, collusion, perjury, racketeering, slavery of all kinds, and state and federal crimes. Watergate (Richard Nixon) and white water (Bill Clinton) are the truth that white-collar crimes can and have gone undetected since the beginning of man's time on our planet. The list goes on forever. Other examples would be the Romans, and Egyptians, slavery in our country and worldwide, World War II with the Germans and against the Jews, and many more like that. The crimes are Russian people killing the Ukraine people and threatening our world. Once again, the United States Government is just standing by and doing nothing for humanity and the people of this country, Ukraine. The first day of the war, anywhere in our world should be stopped immediately. When this country decides to have war still, then the rest of our governments should end the war in that country without a world war.

There are a lot of dirty deeds or criminal actions being done within the United States and around the world. When people come forth with criminal information about government, leaders, secret society, and the rich and powerful, bad things happen to these people who come forward. There is a new type of mafia organization called our government and a secret society in every country. The problems occur on every level of society, from the poor to the rich. Our leaders are not gods; we, the people of each country, endorse our leaders to be in office. When our government does wrong by the people, the constitution laws are written about 2.5 centuries saying impeachment and jail time for criminal action for our leaders, but this never happens or succeeds, as we see with Richard Nixon, Bill Clinton, and many other leaders. The lower levels of society are the ones that pay the price and are set as an example when crimes are committed and end up in our prisons. Do we have equal laws for everybody or different laws for the elite society people? We, the people, need to hold everybody accountable and responsible for their actions or criminal actions no matter the cost of equality for everybody, including our governments and special people. With my cases being on the lower level, we have a town, attorneys, doctors, and judges that should have investigation about my complaints and accusations against all these people involved with my cases. I would not see justice for the crimes that I live through. The people from centuries ago left England and other countries to come to a new land for freedom from a king and taxation, and now we have our government today doing wrong to the people in so many other ways.

CHAPTER 37

History of Mankind

Throughout our world, the history of man has been crude, obnoxious, and archaic; warlike creatures only existed for greed and power from the past time to the present. This part is about how man would take control from the beginning time of man. Man has been and will always be worse than any animals from the past to our presence on our planet, and man is the worst animal of all in our universe. No matter how civilized man becomes, man will always be an animal that destroys himself and many others. In the beginning, men would physically kill each other for their possessions over time. The wars that man created for greed, power, and conquering other tribes, towns, finally kingdoms, and today's world of nations and countries, would become our history throughout our time and world. The kingships and kingdoms from the old countries that ruled our world would fail in time. However, the slavery of conquering other countries to make their kingdoms the most powerful in the world at that time. These problems would continue to our present times and into our future. Unfortunately, we will never have peace and harmony no matter how we all deal with our problems as a world. There will always be someone who wants more power and greed. These reasons are why a man will always kill himself until man is extinct and kills the world as we know our world today. God and the bible say the same thing about the seven sins of the world with men of power and greed. We have a time machine that we all can look into our past, present, and future. We can see all the wars and problems of just one person or a group of people to harm our world, countries, and finally, each individual. We have a passage in the bible that God destroyed our world by a flood because of man's sins and man's wrongdoing. God also destroyed two cities, Sodom and Gomorrah, because of the sexual reason and corruption of men, women, and children. The way the bible was written and God's intentions, God says that he will never interfere with man's life again, but God did say that man will kill himself by fire and burn the world to a cinder. Then there will be a new start for the next generation to start with the innocence of that generation and not the greed and power trip of today's world.

The Bible and God say that three people will try to control the world. Nostradamus, the French astrologer, predicts the presence of man's faults and the end of our world as we know it now. Nostradamus also speaks of three men that will destroy our world, two of them have passed by, but the third one is yet to come into our world; could this be Vladimir Putin? The history of man has always stolen what they wanted for greed and power, and then many other crimes that would follow in the destruction of humanity. Today's world is no better than in the days of the beginning of man. Man would always invent more terrible weapons throughout time, spares, bows and arrows, axes, swords, and final gunpowder with bullets and then bigger bombs like a nuclear bomb. As time went on, ships would sail across the oceans, and the world would grow in time with five oceans and seven continents. When the new world was discovered, this was another time when men would start the hatred, power, and greed would come and only continue with the new continents, North and South America. The lands stolen from America's Indians and the killing of these people would only worsen over time with Africans, Asians, and Indians ' slavery and the killing of these people. There was no justice for the people of that time or people from other countries. People of power and greed took control of North America till the British king wanted more from the people of that time. The American people who controlled this country said no to the British king, which started the Revolutionary War for the freedom of Americans from the king of England.

1776 was the start of this country being established and was an independent country from England, which would start the Revolutionary War. The people of that time would fight for the belief of a better country for the people, but they would only carry their past problems with them to a new country. When America started to expand across the land, the U.S. Army of that time would have multiple wars with Indian nations, the first war with the British and the second war with the native Indians, who were the original owners of this land. It was known at that time that the white man was doing all the crimes against humanity and the people of that time. Slavery would be right behind these problems that the whites would create. The white man pushed religion onto the natives and others and called them barbaric people with no faith or belief. Another war was the Civil War, where the North against the South for the freedom of enslaved people. The problem was also the time of the assassination of President Abraham Lincoln for freeing the enslaved people of that time. The leaders of that time pushed the Irish immigrants and all other immigrants into a civil war for citizenship in our country. The leaders start the wars, and the poor people have to fight. And then have the nation fight for the leaders' rights only and not for the rights of the people and land for freedom. The white man stole the land and people from other countries to profit from greed and power.

Humanity has to cheat, steal, and take advantage of people and situations with greed and power for personal gain and profit. Now we have the two world wars, the first World War 1 with new weapons of mass destruction to the soldiers and citizens and the land. One man and one nation started these problems and led the world into a world war. Then the leaders didn't learn from the first war, so they created a second war with more destructive weapons, an atomic bomb that would level the land of Japan, and not just one bomb but two bombs to destroy the Japanese people. Once again, this war started with the Germans and ended with the fall of three nations and countries. As time passed, we would see more wars with other countries and more weapons that would get more dangerous and deadly. The invention of chemical and biological weapons would be used in the war against the Iraq country. The released poison would affect the people around the war and then around our world, and this would also include nuclear weapons used on Japan and testing in the Pacific Ocean. Now we have power, greed, and personal gain, destroying people over time, with the destruction of the world with nuclear power. The truth from the bible and Nostradamus is becoming more and more accurate in our world.

This world we call Earth is the only place acceptable to our needs of living. Our governments try to go into space and find other planets to live on and conquer. The problems we have on earth with people fighting people and the destruction of our world will not be tolerated by aliens or people from another world. The alien's knowledge and inventions are more incredible than ours here on Earth; the aliens will have more power than us. The possibility of an invasion will be more significant for us if we all think that we will steal other planets from any aliens without consequences. I saw a video warning that we should not venture into space, or there will be consequences from these alien people. They would also explain that the reasons are the destruction we do to our planet and each other. There was another video with the moon landing (1969) to stay out of space so that you cannot be at peace with yourself and others. Our government is socializing with aliens, and then our government lies and says we are the only race in the universe. Anyone with a brain knows that there is something more in our universe than us. A race of animals, reptiles, and people just don't pop up from the dirt or float through space. We all came from somewhere in the universe; the question is where. Remember, we all have only one chance to get things right between ourselves and any other race in our universe. When we make a mistake, you dam all of the world to hell.

CHAPTER 38
Final Health Problems Summary

After seven years of dealing with the lies from Robert Smith and the town of Butland, my two attorneys, Bob Keyhole and Allen Moakley, four main doctors were Primary Dr. Lori Iceburg and Rheumatologist Dr. Peter Orlando with Ph.D. Psychiatrist Dr. Jen Chow and therapist Fay Pain, also Gastrologist Dr. Kenneth Sole and Neurological Dr. Moel Hatcher, then you have the hospitals that the doctors belong to, then you have the two town attorneys Gram Stone and Kerry Dunn, judges; SSI Judge Tony Hare, Federal Judge Dick Shawburg, and the four workmen's comp. Case Judges Jill Ripoff, case judge Betty Macduff, senior judge Bill Child, and mediation judge John Mack. One or all of these people could have corrected these problems at any time, in accordance with our laws. The witnesses could have come forward without consequences to their job or them being covered up as witnesses by the town, attorneys, or judges. A family and girlfriend supported the truth of what they saw and knew about the crimes committed in these cases, plus understanding my health problems. My family and girlfriend supported the fact of me fighting these problems and people till I had nothing to prove. I follow the laws by writing complaints and reporting to all the proper legal authorities with no results from anyone involved.

The health problems started with stomach pains and grew from them, with stress being behind all the problems that the doctors couldn't admit on a legal level. The next problem was anxiety and IBS problems aggravated by someone and added to stress-related problems. The secondary problems from anxiety and IBS are chest pain, headaches, body aches, confusion with mind and body surrounding my body, paranoia and phobias, avoidance behavior, stomach cramps, constipation, and diarrhea. The third main problem was fibromyalgia, but arthritis from the jobs that were performed over the years would only add more pain to the fibromyalgia. These problems of fibromyalgia and IBS were lifelong problems that I would never get a cure from with the rest of my life. The one problem I had before the town was IBS from the peanut butter case in 2008, and arthritis has been from working over the years. Fibromyalgia is a medical problem that has a lot of converse from the doctors, but when you have the C.D.C. explaining all the problems of fibromyalgia and the doctors are just ignoring the medical problem, that only increases all of the stress problems to the maximum levels of stress. Then the doctors do not cooperate with the attorneys and judges, and the laws only increase the stress levels higher with any person's life. All of this stress would eventually lead to PTSD (post-traumatic stress disorder) from the start that all my doctors never conceived of, my attorney Allen the town attorneys, and all the judges. PTSD has its side effects, which also work against all the stress problems I have explained. Fibromyalgia has the same and different problems, which are body aches, headaches, fogginess, muscle cramps, and pains; the nervous system has been compromised because of fibromyalgia and other conditions, chest pains can also affect the body organs, and toward the end can leave you in a wheelchair or bedridden with death coming sooner than later.

As the years go on with these problems and lots of pain increases, it starts to affect more parts of the body, especially the nervous system sending messages of pain running through your body. A better way to explain it is that your lights are turned on forever and eventually burn out like an electrical system (Dr. Peter Orlando explains). When these problems started happening, I started having problems with the spinal cord, which carries the two main systems in your body one blood system and the other is your nervous system. When it came to my spinal problems, my spine was compromised in three spots or areas the neck, mid-back, and tailbone. This problem would be happening without me working at all; this would occur over time after seven years of dealing with the cases.

Another problem was that my hip sockets were failing; my bone was cut like a diamond from how Dr. Peter explained the x-rays and what was seen. I would have complained about my hands and feet pain to Primary Lori Iceberg and Rheumatologist Peter Orlando, and these problems would just be ignored. It's no different from the diagnosis and prognosis of all the doctors with no complete answers to my health problems myself and the cases with attorney Allen and the others. A man in his 50s without working for seven years, expects me to go back to work with all the health problems and the new health problems they can't explain to me or the law (people). Which is needed from a doctor to prove any case in our country, the doctors are the key factor in establishing medical problems.

The pain from the fibromyalgia in my hands and feet and spinal cord have pain that is so bad and unexplainable in words. I'll start with my hands in describing the pain and problems; there is no feeling in my hands, numbness, stabbing pain, coldness, feeling of someone is pulling my joints apart in the hands, with the palms feeling like a hammer smashing my palms of my hands, itchiness, muscle spasm and feels like something is walking on my body everywhere and when there is nothing there when the weather changes to rain, snow, and cold temperature, my hands, feet, and spinal cord all acts up with pain and other problems. The only time I may have an ok day is summertime when the days are warm, but when the night comes or bad weather, I go into a battle with my body being in pain. All of these problems of pain are the same between hands and feet. The spinal cord is another story, especially when the doctors finally listened to me about multiple MRIs of my neck, middle back, tailbone, and hips. When doctors found problems with these areas, the doctors did nothing about it with the finding of my neck, back, and hips. Somehow, fibromyalgia affected the nervous system and spinal cord, and the weather would kill me every time it came. When the record showed the wrong problems with my neck, back, and hips, my attorney or judges were never notified about new health problems. The spinal cord would act up, and I would get headaches, dizziness, and fatigue with all pain and dizziness. At the end of all medical and legal procedures, the medical was never complete or corrected. The legal side never had any proper information from the medical records and original complaints from my doctors or me. All the judges made a wrong judgment from the false information in documents and lies about the complete case records (actual complaints, medical records, legal records).

The pain and nightmares would also cause problems with my sleeping, eating, and weight gain and would only worsen over time for seven years. All the doctors were told about my sleeping, eating, and weight gain problems; the medical records show the weight gain. When visiting the doctors, they also noticed my eyes and asked if I was sleeping correctly, and my answers were always no to the doctors. When any new problems about my health came up, nobody ever got notified, starting with each doctor, attorney, and judge. My attorney Allen never requested my records from all the doctors, and they never had an updated document in front of them. In accordance with Workmen's Comp. laws, you need a 6-month review from all the doctors to see if the health problems are continued, and the attorneys and judges never got these updated records. As a result, I have all types of pain and issues with getting around and not having a normal life doing household chores and everyday life.

Dark Justice White Collar Crimes

CHAPTER 39
Final Thoughts

The health conditions I suffered during my seven years of legal battles have worsened over the years, and new conditions have developed. I don't think my doctors followed their Hippocratic oath or practiced proper protocol. And they didn't follow the law.

Many people I've shared my story with have told me that I should never have had to suffer such devastating mental and physical issues. Many agreed with me that medical and legal professionals and the many people I wrote to ask for help had taken advantage of my situation. I never got the help and support I needed from those who had the power to give it to me. They looked the other way when I desperately needed them. I felt like a solitary man up against a bunch of bullies. When politicians campaign for office, they say what the voters want to hear. Most people don't realize—or don't want to know— that they are lying and avoiding the issues. They care about their constituents or their problems. Once they are in office, everything they said in those fine speeches flies out the window while they sign up for kickbacks and plan their re-election strategies. The COVID-19 pandemic is a good example. The government shut down the world, but the rich and powerful had enough money so their lives didn't change much. Those with fewer monetary resources struggled to survive, both financially and emotionally and No one needs the problems that arise when people make things harder than they should be.

For years I've heard people say that this is the only government and legal system we have, and we need laws so we can maintain order among the people. It is time to make changes in our government, and there cannot be any questions from the politicians. Remember, we elect, support, and pay our government officials through our taxes. Is the present chaotic state of our government the thanks we get from our government? The people of the United States should take back this from those who are abusing their power, and they should hold the politicians and other officials responsible for their actions. My journey has come to an end—for now. I am so grateful for my family members, my girlfriend, and the people who showed me kindness along the way even though they were unable to help me.

As I bring my book to a close, I want to stress to everyone reading this book to feel the heart of my story and know how important it is to take action against the white-collar crimes that plague our modern world. Throughout my account, I've meticulously detailed the heinous offenses of perjury and deceit, the sinister manipulation of justice, and the alarming tampering with medical and legal records.

My earnest plea is for workers to muster the courage to stand in solidarity with their colleagues when they witness the truth. Everyone must step forward, to bring these issues to the attention of law enforcement, and refuse to be complicit in the face of corruption. I've brought these concerns to our elected officials and the various legal agencies, urging them to heed the cries of those affected by white-collar crimes, to take cognizance of their grievances, and to champion the cause of justice for the people.

White-collar crimes often evade the spotlight because they lack the sensationalism of violent offenses, yet their consequences can be just as cataclysmic, manifesting in physical and mental anguish for the victims. Mental stress, in particular, emerges as a silent perpetrator, an instigator of various maladies in the human body, from the relentless grip of fibromyalgia to the suffocating tendrils of anxiety, neuropathy, and irritable bowel syndrome (IBS).

It is very clear to me that there is a disconnect between our medical and justice systems, and if left unaddressed, threatens to ruin our world. In these closing pages, I hope all who read this book join me in exposing white-collar crimes so they are met with the scrutiny they so rightfully deserve. The hope of my book, my story, is that together, we can shed light on the darkness that surrounds these offenses, ultimately creating a world where justice prevails, and the welfare of the people takes priority over anything else.

www.ingramcontent.com/pod-product-compliance
Lightning Source LLC
Chambersburg PA
CBHW060453030426
42337CB00015B/1576